MORE THAN
A HOBBY

MORE THAN A HOBBY

How a $600 Start-up Became America's Home & Craft Superstore

DAVID GREEN
WITH DEAN MERRILL

THOMAS NELSON
Since 1798

NASHVILLE   DALLAS   MEXICO CITY   RIO DE JANEIRO

Published in Nashville, Tennessee, by Thomas Nelson. Thomas Nelson is a registered trademark of Thomas Nelson, Inc.

Thomas Nelson, Inc., titles may be purchased in bulk for educational, business, fund-raising, or sales promotional use. For information, please e-mail SpecialMarkets@ThomasNelson.com.

Scripture quotations are from the HOLY BIBLE, NEW INTERNATIONAL VERSION®. © 1973, 1978, 1984 by International Bible Society. Used by permission of Zondervan Publishing House. All rights reserved.

Published in association with the literary agency of Mark Sweeney & Associates, 641 Old Hickory Blvd., Suite 416, Brentwood, Tennessee 37027.

ISBN 978-1-59555-983-8 (TP)

Library of Congress Cataloging-in-Publication Data

Green, David, 1941 Nov. 13-
    More than a hobby : How a $600 Startup Became America's Home-and-Craft Superstore / David Green with Dean Merrill.
      p. cm.
Includes bibliographical references.
    ISBN 0-7852-0831-3 (hardcover)
    1. Retail trade—Management. 2. Entrepreneurship. I. Merrill, Dean. II. Title.
    HF5429.G6792 2005
    658.8'7—dc22

2005000098

Printed in the United States of America

10 11 12 13 14 LSI 5 4 3 2 1

I dedicate this book to three ladies:
my mother, Marie, the inspiration of my life;
my wife, Barbara, the love of my life;
and my daughter and personal cheerleader,
Darsee, the light of my life.
I also dedicate it to my two sons, Mart and Steven,
whom I love dearly and hold in the utmost respect;
to my nine grandchildren, the joys of my life:
Brent, David T., Derek, Scott,
Lauren, Amy, Lindy, Danielle, and little Grace;
to my son-in-law, Stan,
whom God created especially for my daughter;
and to my two daughters-in-law, Diana and Jackie,
whom I call super-moms.
Because of their past and continued support and prayers,
my life has been fulfilled.

CONTENTS

⟿

CHAPTER 1

WHY I LOVE RETAIL

———— ⸎ ————

You could smell the fresh popcorn as soon as you came through the front doors of McClellan's five-and-dime on Hudson Street. The wooden floors creaked as you stepped toward the candy counter to the left or the toiletries department to the right, where a smiling young clerk would say, "Good morning!" as she waited to serve you.

If you passed by a little farther, you came to the second bank of counters. Sheets and towels were overseen by an older lady named Mrs. Duncan, while the toy department was enlivened by petite, energetic Ann, who was ready to kneel down and give any young boy or girl a squeeze. Nearby were the hosiery and lingerie sections, and on toward the back of the store came housewares, hardware, and pets. In charge of it all was a wiry, medium-height manager in his late fifties, Mr. T. Texas Tyler, who was always on the move.

McClellan's sat on the east side of the courthouse square of Altus, Oklahoma, a county-seat town of some 20,000 in the middle of cotton fields and cattle ranches 220 miles northwest of Dallas. Not that our family came to shop very often at McClellan's; we simply didn't have the money. My father was the pastor of a church with no more than thirty-five attendees, which meant a tiny salary despite the need to put food on the table for six kids. We had no car; we just walked wherever we needed to go. Aunts and cousins from California would occasionally send us hand-me-down clothes, which helped a great deal. That way our parents only had to fill in the socks and underwear.

The church people were as gracious as they could be, supplementing the meager collection funds with weekly "poundings"—a time in the service when they would bring vegetables, fruit, or other foodstuffs (sometimes by the *pound*—hence, the name) to the altar to help the pastor's family along. My mother accepted them all with warm appreciation. Still, we went weeks at a time without meat on our supper table. The idea of having an extra quarter or 50 cents we could spend at McClellan's was far beyond our reality.

As a result, it's little wonder that I didn't feel comfortable at Altus High School, in the swirl of students my age who had new clothes and money for snacks. I was the kid off to the side, the kid washing dishes in the cafeteria in order to earn a lunch pass. It's hard for me to remember any friends in high school. I'd already had to repeat seventh grade, and whenever I was required to stand up and give an oral report in front of the class, I froze in my seat. I simply couldn't muster the courage.

"David," the teacher would quietly say to me, "I'm sorry, but you must do this. If you refuse, I will have no choice but to give you an F."

Under those conditions, I would definitely take the F. I

still hadn't recovered from the time a while back when I had mispronounced the word *the*, and everybody laughed. It was something about "the oven" or "the Industrial Revolution," and I had said *thuh* instead of *thee*. My classmates thought that was hilarious.

So with a heavy sigh, my teacher would murmur, "Okay, you come back at the end of school today and give your report just to me, with no one else in the room." That I was willing to do.

When I enrolled for my junior year in the fall of 1958, something absolutely wonderful happened. There on the class list was something called "D.E."—Distributive Education (more commonly called Work-Study today). "What is that?" I wanted to know.

"Well, businesses in town call in to offer part-time jobs for students," a young teacher named J. W. Weatherford explained, "and you get to leave during the school day to go work. You still get credit for the class, and you earn money along the way."

I was thrilled with this combination. I quickly signed up for the D.E. class. And that's how I entered the world of retail.

⌇⌇

The first day that I left school at ten-thirty and walked the mile to McClellan's, I was as excited as I'd ever been. "Welcome, son," Mr. Tyler greeted me. "To get started, you go grab the yarn broom back there and sweep the floor." This was dusty Oklahoma, after all, and the aisles needed attention several times a day. He taught me to sweep with a compound of sawdust with some light oil mixed in.

When that was finished, Mr. Tyler said, "All right, now let's go upstairs to the stockroom. I'll show you how to check in the merchandise that just arrived." We went up to a room on the second floor where there were bins for each department and a long worktable for unpacking the cartons that the trucks delivered to our little 5,000-square-foot store. I saw the conveyor belt that chugged upstairs to the stockroom from the freight dock in the back. I saw the hand-crank machine that turned out price stickers so we could mark the merchandise before the ladies took it downstairs to display. Yes, price stickers; this was long before the days of bar coding, and few items were prepriced by the suppliers.

That evening, after I walked the mile back to our house across the tracks, I excitedly told my mother about my day. "Now that I have a *real* job," I announced, "I'm going to buy you something really nice!" I had worked alongside her and my brothers and sisters in the cotton fields for years to get money for our family. But this job at the five-and-dime was at a whole new level. I'd much rather be doing this than sports or clubs after school.

As a stock boy, I always carried two tools in my pocket: a case knife and a glass cutter. The second of these was because we were always making new bins on the countertops for individual items. Whereas today you might buy buttons or pencils in card packets that hang on wall pegs, back then items were offered in bulk, and customers picked out as many as they needed. Making the bins inevitably created lots and lots of leftover glass pieces. These congregated into a jumble in a space under the staircase, along with the various clips that held the panels together.

I took it upon myself to sort these glass remnants by size and bring order to the chaos. If I gathered all the three-inch pieces together, then the four-inch pieces, the five-inch pieces, and so on, they could be put to use again, instead of someone wastefully cutting into a large sheet of glass for just a small panel. It was a challenge that I somehow found to be fun.

I quickly fell into the rhythm of working forty hours a week, or even more. Three of my teachers eventually called me in to say that while my aptitude tests showed potential, my grades weren't matching up. "Do you work or something?" one of them said.

With a smart-aleck attitude I responded, "Yeah, I probably work more hours than you do!" It's a wonder I didn't get suspended for that.

But retail was such a joyous contrast to the rest of my life. I had finally found something I was good at. Whenever I came to work, things were bustling. For instance, we cooked all of our own nuts for sale: Spanish peanuts, walnuts, cashews, hazelnuts. Spanish peanuts were 29 cents a pound. Also, there was bin after bin of orange slices and candy corn and coconut bonbons—it was a great atmosphere.

The Officers Club out at Altus Air Force Base would occasionally stop by with a huge order: two hundred pounds of mixed nuts. That meant I got to work at night cooking up large quantities of cashews, hazelnuts, and others, mixing them with oil in a big tub.

In the fall of the year, migrant workers would arrive to pick the area's cotton, and on Saturdays they would inevitably gravitate toward our store. I was busier than ever filling the counters with merchandise, seeing it go out the front door, and refilling the counters. We loaded up on blankets—a dollar apiece—especially for the migrants, and sold a ton of them.

I studied what Mr. Tyler did. A lot of his work, I realized, was being a great organizer. He also knew the details of merchandise; he had an innate sense for what people would be willing to buy. The more I watched, the more I became convinced that I could be a store manager. I could be successful after all! This became my goal.

I didn't wait on customers myself; they intimidated me. The men's clothing store next door to McClellan's tried to hire me one time, promising more money than I was presently making. But that would have meant dealing with customers, which scared me to death. So I stayed put, doing the physical labor at the five-and-dime so other people could make sales.

One time I was attempting to clean toilets, hardly touching the porcelain because I found the job distasteful, when Mr. Tyler came by. "Look, son—you have to do this job right!" he scolded as he plunged his bare hand into the toilet bowl and vigorously swished the cleanser around. I was amazed. He was a stickler for thoroughness, for organization, for detail.

More than once I saw him follow along after a customer who had put out a cigarette butt under his shoe. Mr. Tyler would reach down, pick up the butt with his hand, and put it into his pocket. Again, I could hardly believe my eyes. But he would not tolerate a sloppy store in any way.

He began training me in how to display merchandise attractively. In time I got to trim the display windows in the front. To me, a store window was like a painter's canvas, with all the possibilities in the world. This work usually happened at night, because you had to get into awkward spaces, and you could spread out your items in the aisles as you worked.

One evening a few weeks before Easter, I made the mistake of building the display around chocolate bunnies. It looked very nice—until the hot sun hit the window the next afternoon. What a dumb idea. But in time, I got better at the job.

Mr. Tyler would take me down to the corner drugstore sometimes just to talk about the business. He'd drink coffee while I had a Coke, and he would pass along his wisdom. He'd update me on whether sales were growing or slipping. Sitting at that counter, I learned the fascinating concept of markup: that a store could buy something for 10 cents and sell it for 20, thus providing employment for the staff, and paying for the store's lights and heat and rent and insurance—and maybe even having a penny left over in the end. Wow! Here was a way to make real money.

I began to see that in retail, the sky was the limit. You could always open more stores, or expand the stores you had; there was no end. I found this tremendously inspiring.

I never second-guessed my entrance into retail. I knew from day one that this was the way for me to go. *I can become a manager . . . then a district supervisor . . . and maybe someday even start a business of my own.*

Obviously, I had not the slightest dream of what Hobby Lobby has become today: a chain of more than three hundred stores that gross a total $1.4 billion a year in sales. At that point, I was just excited to be making 60 cents an hour. I spent most of it on furniture for our home. I bought my mother a complete dining set, a sofa, and a refrigerator. There was nothing I would rather do with my earnings than give them away.

I did splurge a little, however, on a pretty, young part-timer in the stationery department, taking her across the street to the drugstore for a 5-cent Coke. If I was feeling really rich, we'd add a 5-cent ice-cream cone to the deal. Total outlay for the two of us: 20 cents. Today that young clerk is my wife, Barbara, who deserves as much credit for Hobby Lobby's growth and success as anyone.

My first big purchase was a 1951 Ford, for which I paid about $200. Later, I noticed that Barbara's current boyfriend drove a convertible, and I decided I needed to upgrade in order to compete for her attention. So I bought a yellow 1953 Ford convertible without even looking under the hood. It turned out to be the lemon that its color indicated.

From the very beginning, I loved the work—and that's an important point: To succeed in retail, you have to love it. The process of bringing items in, displaying them attractively, and seeing them miraculously change into actual cash in the drawer has to get your blood racing.

> **FROM THE VERY BEGINNING, I LOVED THE WORK—AND THAT'S AN IMPORTANT POINT: TO SUCCEED IN RETAIL, YOU HAVE TO LOVE IT.**

You can triple the sale of an item just by how and where you display it. It's some of the greatest fun in the world. There's no way a corporate office should tell a local manager how to display every little thing. At Hobby Lobby we give some guidance, some photos of attractive merchandising, but the real magic happens at the store level. And when you see the results each month in your profit-and-loss statement, it can be very exciting.

I managed to squeak through high school and enlisted in the Air Force Reserve. After six weeks of basic training, I was assigned to Sheppard Air Force Base in Wichita Falls, Texas—not all that far from Altus. I hitchhiked home to see Barbara every weekend I could.

As soon as active duty was over, I returned to my job at McClellan's. Barbara and I were married the following February; I was nineteen years old, and she was just seventeen. Her parents weren't involved in retail; her dad was a heavy-equipment mechanic who worked for the county. But her parents could see that I loved my chosen field and brought a good work ethic to it, so they felt sure I would provide for their daughter.

A year later I began working for another five-and-dime chain called TG&Y, which was expanding much faster. It was the Wal-Mart of that era, adding thirty to forty stores a year, and I definitely wanted one of those manager spots. I got my wish in Oklahoma City when I was only twenty-one. The store was small, just 4,000 square feet with six employees. But here was a chance to show what I could do.

More promotions came along during the next decade as I learned the dynamics of retail management. It was a good time both at work and at home. Our two sons, Mart and Steve, were born, and a few years later we adopted a wonderful little girl we named Darsee.

Then in 1970 we started our own business. I saw potential that TG&Y was not capturing. In my sizable family-center store, for example, I grew the pet department to thirteen employees, a highly unusual thing. We had rows and rows of saltwater fish, freshwater fish, birds, hamsters, and other creatures to delight the customers—especially children. And when you get children liking your store, the moms follow.

I brought in truckloads of ten-gallon fish tanks and put them on sale for an incredibly low price—lower than the going wholesale price, in fact. Why? Because once someone buys a fish tank, he has to put stuff in it: the fish, the gravel, the pump, and all the other paraphernalia. That's where we could make our money.

A talented young man named John Seward was my pet department supervisor (he later came to join me in the Hobby Lobby venture). At times the TG&Y pet buyer at the home office would call us to find better sources. All of this was showing me what could be done with specializing, even within a general-merchandise operation.

I thought the same thing could happen with the crafts department. My only problem was a lack of start-up money. So a friend named Larry Pico and I borrowed $600 from the bank, bought a frame chopper, and began making miniature picture frames on the kitchen table for wholesaling. Actually, I didn't glue nearly as many frames as Barbara and the boys did; we paid the little guys 7 cents per frame.

The goal for Barbara and me was truly not to make a lot of money; it was to be successful at this challenge. Soon the orders started to come, so many that Barbara had to go out in search of more workers. She found them at the local Cerebral Palsy Center, where victims of that disorder could do this kind of work quite well.

Two years later we opened our first Hobby Lobby near the state capitol building, a tiny 300-square-foot arts-and-crafts store (think of the size of a large master bedroom). I still kept my TG&Y job for another three years, until we were sure we could make it. Today I'm the chairman of eight different affiliated companies as well as the CEO of Hobby Lobby, but the thing I like to do the *least* is sit behind a desk. Within a couple of miles of our headquarters is a Hobby Lobby store, and I find myself there almost every day I'm in town. Why? It helps me stay close to retailing.

Another thing I don't have to mess with is dealing with stockholders and all the federal and state paperwork of being a public company. We're still family-owned, which keeps life a whole lot simpler. When my wife and kids and I decide to make a business move, we don't have to ask Wall Street about it.

WE'RE STILL FAMILY-OWNED, WHICH KEEPS LIFE A WHOLE LOT SIMPLER.

Unlike most companies, we have no vice president of merchandising. That's my job. Yes, we have eight merchandise managers who oversee our thirty-six buyers. But when it comes to home accents, I'm the merchandise manager myself. In fact, I'm the actual buyer of a lot of those items. That's the most exciting part of my work.

Retailing, at least in my personal view, has four keys. And the sequence is important. They are:

1. Run your business in harmony with God's laws. This will keep you on an ethical footing. Seek to please God in everything you do.

2. Focus on people more than money. Without employees and customers, you're going nowhere.

Make sure you never stop thinking about the customer's perspective. And make sure you have the right people at the helm of each area.

3. Be a *merchant*. Notice, I didn't just say "business-person." That's too generic. Your core activity is *buying and selling merchandise*. That's what it's all about. The rest is periphery, or even distraction.

4. Install the proper systems to support the first three keys.

I love the fact that retailing is very competitive. I never got the chance to play sports in school, but the retail world is as competitive as any football league.

Every new year sees huge retail companies fall, despite their high-priced consultants and sophisticated marketing research. Retailing is difficult—that's what makes it exciting for me.

In 2001 we started a new spin-off company, a high-end home furnishings store called Hemispheres. Besides sofas and tables, we carry framed art, Oriental rugs, and row upon row of mirrors and lamps. For the outdoors, we provide patio furniture, fountains, and large planters—all at value prices. I know that my odds of succeeding with this venture are only one out of ten; 90 percent of start-ups in this field don't make it. I fully intend to be in the 10 percent! So far we're losing money, but we're learning a great deal, and we're pushing to get the sales volumes up and the margins up. This is my sport.

What if we in retail had sportscasters doing the play-by-play on our efforts? "David Green just made a brilliant buy on decorative baskets—but look out, he's going to mess up in the way he's pricing them . . ." Maybe we need to see ourselves under such a spotlight. We need to watch the instant replays and see in living color where we went wrong.

I want to be the very best competitor I can be. The Bible says, "Whatever your hand finds to do, do it with all your might, for in the grave, where you are going, there is neither working nor planning nor knowledge nor wisdom" (Ecclesiastes 9:10).

At the same time, we ask that all employees see themselves as servants. Our stores serve the customers. Yes, Hobby Lobby is considered to be a "self-serve" operation. But some departments do require service, and whenever a customer anywhere has a question, we need to be there for them.

Similarly, at the corporate office, we ask that our people be servants to the stores. We exist to help the stores succeed. The warehouse and the corporate office are supposed to make things convenient for the stores, not the other way around. If I find that someone is not helping out when asked, or is belittling a store manager off in Minnesota, I deal with that person right away.

> **THE WAREHOUSE AND THE CORPORATE OFFICE ARE SUPPOSED TO MAKE THINGS CONVENIENT FOR THE STORES, NOT THE OTHER WAY AROUND.**

If everything is working as it should, the staff will feel honored and fulfilled, and customers will be pleased. We've actually had first-time customers walk into a Hobby Lobby and exclaim, "I think I've just died and gone to heaven!"

One couple told us that they were looking at houses to buy, found two that they liked, and chose one over the other solely because it was closer to a Hobby Lobby.

In what other line of work could you have this much fun?

∽

This book is not meant to be my life story—I'm not a celebrity, and I have no desire to be one. I've always brushed aside the occasional compliment that some people give: "You ought to write a book!" I wasn't interested in glorifying myself.

Instead, this book will take you into the unique company that Hobby Lobby has become. I'll try to show you how it works, how we work to serve our customers, and why we sometimes go against the grain of American business practice. I also want you to see, in the later chapters, what motivates my family and me to do what we do. I hope you enjoy the ride.

PART ONE

OUT FRONT

CHAPTER 2

A CREATIVE FRENZY

—————— ꢍ ——————

To explain what makes Hobby Lobby tick, I'll start this section of the book with the obvious things that appeal to everyday customers. After all, if customers don't find enjoyment and satisfaction by coming into your store, it won't matter if you have the greatest, fanciest, most sophisticated business model in the world. I'm not into complicated theories; I just get up every morning and say, "What are home-and-craft customers looking for today, and how can I provide it to them?"

The target customer for me is a woman who wants to make her home better in some way. Yes, men shop at Hobby Lobby, too, but the overwhelming majority are female. They may be interested in making an item themselves, or they may want to buy it ready to use. Either way, their goal is to create a more attractive, beautiful place to live.

What does this kind of woman want when she goes shopping? First of all, she appreciates a wide *selection* of interesting merchandise, so that's our topic for this chapter. She also wants to enjoy the *shopping experience*; we'll talk about that next. And of course, she doesn't want to pay any more than she has to. Therefore, the subject of chapter 4 is *pricing*.

We'll get into the interior gears and pulleys of retail operation later on. But first things first.

Take a stroll through any Hobby Lobby, and you'll lose all track of time (at least I hope you will) among the panorama of items for your home, from lampshades to cookie tins to teddy bears; gift bags; plastic tablecovers, both round and rectangular, in twenty different colors, each with matching crepe paper; U.S. flags (small, medium, large); clock-face numerals; glue guns for your craft projects; Styrofoam hearts; acid-free scrapbook paper; bare-wood shelving; posterboard; wall sconces; pinking shears; clay flowerpots; rubber stamps with a happy face that says "Super Job"; and the list goes on.

Time after time, surveys of our customers tell us they come to Hobby Lobby most of all for the amazing selection. Newcomers walk in the front door and don't get halfway to the back wall before uttering, "My goodness—this place has *everything*!"

That's exactly the reaction our company's creative director (who happens to be my daughter, Darsee) is seeking. She calls it a *creative frenzy*. "Nobody brings together so many unique things under one roof," she says.

In a year's time, we offer approximately 100,000 different items. Slightly more than 46,000 of these are on display year-round; the other 50,000 or so are seasonal or onetime items.

During the course of a year at Hobby Lobby, you will see approximately 50,000 *new* items. That is because of two practices:

1. About a fifth of the year-round items (more than 9,000) are retired and replaced every year. We're constantly purging the warehouse of items whose sales pattern is slowing. Meanwhile, new items, as well as new colors, new styles, and new sizes, are always coming online.

2. About four-fifths of the seasonal and onetime items (some 40,000 of them) won't be repeated next time around.

Put the two groups together, and you have nearly 50,000 items you didn't see a year ago.

We call the standing warehouse items "pull items"; the stores continually pull them into their facilities to offer their customers. The seasonals and onetimers, on the other hand, we call "push items"; we in the home office in Oklahoma City make the decision to push them into the stores for a given period.

Every week, a store manager fills out his or her "pull" order. A computer printout lists all 46,000 items and tells how many of each should be on hand in that store to constitute a two-month supply. If the store's stock is below that number, it should reorder. Within twenty-four hours (or forty-eight at the most), a truck will show up with that merchandise, so the store doesn't even come close to running out.

PARTS AND PIECES

The average store has $1.2 million worth of inventory under its roof at any one time—that's our cost, not the sticker price. Of all the standing items, more than half will sell only one or two a month in the average store. In other words, we're not a mass merchandiser, the kind of store that sells a ton of a relatively few number of items—say, disposable diapers, toothpaste, or potato chips. We're the opposite: We're a specialty store that sells ones and twos and threes of a ton of different items.

I got a shocking reminder of how many items we carry the afternoon of May 27, 1984, when our first Tulsa store got flooded out. A sudden downpour during the night had overwhelmed a creek that ran behind our 55,000-square-foot store, filling the aisles with up to three feet of water.

I was getting ready for church that Sunday morning when the call came. Soon Barbara and I, along with our kids, were on the turnpike and driving the one hundred miles northeast to Tulsa.

What a sight unfolded before us when we drove up. The parking lot was filled with soggy merchandise—everything from bolts of fabric to tote bags to floral displays. Employees and even some of their spouses were already hard at work. My heart sank.

Inside the store, employees and kindhearted volunteers were sweeping water toward the doors. I even saw small fish in the aisles! I knew our insurance policy, like most, didn't cover floods. Meanwhile, Hobby Lobby's finances were stretched due to recent expansion—we were up to eleven stores at that point. Putting all this back together was going to be a huge task.

But in time, we reopened the doors of the Tulsa store for business once again. (One unusual move I made was to write every vendor and ask if, in light of our setback, they could help us with a 10 percent credit against any of our outstanding invoices. They stepped up wonderfully; as a result, we saved more than $300,000. Today, two decades later, a plaque still hangs on our home office wall listing each vendor who helped us out.)

To serve customers in the home decorating and crafting area, you simply have to have a wide selection. A few years back, Sam Walton opened five craft stores called Helen's (named after his wife). Before long, he found it so different, so opposite to the Wal-Mart model, he got out of the field.

A craft store is in "the parts business." If a woman wants to do a project that requires ten parts, and Hobby Lobby has only eight of them, she's going to give up in frustration. We have to carry all ten parts.

In mass merchandising, price is everything. The cheaper the Crest toothpaste, the better. In crafts, price is still important—but not as important as selection. You can have the world's most amazing bargain on purple sequins, but if the customer doesn't want purple, she's not going to buy them. She's more interested in finding the sea-green sequins she had in mind.

No other craft chain I know of comes close to carrying 46,000 items in its warehouse. We see the larger selection as absolutely necessary, even though it requires extra work, organization, and money. It means breaking down the suppliers' packs into very small numbers. If, for example, a supplier ships us a certain color of silk flowers in packs of forty-eight each, that could be a year's supply in one of our stores. We can't insist that the store swallow that much. So what's the option? Dump the item altogether? No, the option is to break apart the pack in our warehouse in order to ship out realistic quantities.

This means thinking about what's best for the customer

and the individual store, not what's easiest for the central warehouse. Anything we can do to help the store and make things work, we must do, no matter how cumbersome it is. In the long run, it pays dividends.

STARTING SMALL

I still can remember when we opened our first retail store back in 1972. We didn't have all the departments we have today; it was just crafts (beads, sequins) and a few art supplies, such as our miniature frames. The entire inventory was less than $3,000. It wasn't enough to merit the doors being open; Barbara recalls days when just one or two customers would stop by. Obviously, we weren't making any net income from retailing. Only the frame-making operation paid the bills.

> THE LONG-HAIRED HIPPIES OF THAT ERA WOULD COME INTO OUR STORE AND SIT DOWN ON THE CARPET TO STRING TOGETHER BEADS OF VARIOUS COLORS, PICKING THEM OUT OF BINS ONE AT A TIME.

A year later, we moved to an old house that gave us maybe 1,000 square feet. Here we could expand our merchandise. Neighborhood residents starting coming by. The long-haired hippies of that era would come into our store and sit down on the carpet to string together beads of various colors, picking them out of bins one at a time. That was because we offered a good selection even in our limited product lines.

Today we have the following departments:

— Art supplies
— Crafts
— Frames
— Candles
— Needlework
— Fabric
— Baskets
— Floral
— Card and party items
— Home accents—everything from wall pieces to throw pillows
— Seasonal (Valentine's Day, St. Patrick's, Easter, Mother's and Father's Days, Fourth of July, autumn, Halloween, Thanksgiving, Christmas)
— Hobbies—everything from plastic models to trains to science projects
— Garden
— Small furniture
— Memory (scrapbooking)
— Wearable art
— Jewelry-making

One of my jobs as CEO is to keep the big picture in mind, allotting the square footage to each department for the best overall results. Some departments flourish for a time, then seem to sag, and so I cut back their allotted space for something else.

Our purchasing agents, or buyers, are always finding exciting new things they want to add to the stores. I share their excitement—but then I also have to ask, "Where will we get the additional space? What category are we going to shrink to make room for this hot new line?"

Sometimes the answer comes from analyzing sales data. Our floral department, for example, used to be 12 percent of our total business; more recently, it's down to around 6 percent. For one thing, we've had to endure adverse publicity from the home-decorating gurus. Martha Stewart, for example, says: "Get rid of those silk flowers! Use fresh flowers instead." Popular TV shows such as *Trading Spaces* frequently say, when moving in to redecorate an older home, "Okay, first thing, throw out that wreath with the artificial flowers . . ."

But we don't give up altogether. Not every homemaker is going to do what the gurus say. I may cut back the floral space in our stores somewhat to make room for something else. But over the years, I've learned a few tactics to keep going in the face of a headwind. When a product is frowned upon, for whatever reason, I *don't* cut prices. That just reinforces the bad vibrations. Instead, I believe in trading *up*. Our buyers go out and find a better product that we can offer for a *higher* price. We give the customer a reason to come back and take a fresh look at this item or category. In time, the sales trend can turn around.

One of our most enduring categories is the product line that started it all for Barbara and me: frames. The small picture frames we made in the beginning were strictly a craft item. Customers would use them to hold small paintings for a grouping on the wall.

Then a wholesale company (the same one that sold us that first frame-chopper machine) wanted to get out of the ready-made frame business. The owner sold us a forty-foot truckload of inventory for $2,000. We had no way to store this much in our small facility, so we parked the trailer out front and began running newspaper ads for a big sale. We spread some frames out on the lawn, while the rest could be seen by climbing up a ladder into the back of the trailer. (Fortunately, nobody slipped and fell and sued us!)

It turned out to be a tremendous success; we netted five or six times our investment. So we bought another truckload for $4,000, and a third for $8,000, still managing to be profitable.

This showed us the potential of large, ready-made frames. It's still one of our mainstays. Today we stock every size from 2 x 3 inches to 24 x 36 inches. Granted, frames consume a lot of floor space, and they come in lots of different styles. But people will always want to hang a picture of their child or their mother on the wall, and Hobby Lobby will always be there to help them.

> WHEN A PRODUCT IS FROWNED UPON, FOR WHATEVER REASON, I DON'T CUT PRICES. THAT JUST REINFORCES THE BAD VIBRATIONS. INSTEAD, I BELIEVE IN TRADING UP.

Our most popular frame style is the rustic, unfinished wood we call "barnwood." People have a soft spot for the past, it seems—for simpler days, for their rural roots. So they put country scenes in these frames . . . paintings of old-time kitchens, for example. The barnwood line is perfect for this.

I'll let you in on a little secret: The wood in these frames doesn't come from barns. It comes from old picket fences that are being replaced! The fence companies are more than happy to give us the old, weathered, paint-peeling wood that they otherwise would have to haul to the city dump and pay a fee to get rid of it. We take it off their hands, put it through our specially calibrated router machines, and glue it into frames for people to buy.

NOT EVERYTHING BELONGS

It took us a while to figure out what belongs in a Hobby Lobby and what does not. We learned the hard way, for example, that we didn't want to carry radio-controlled airplanes as part of our hobby section. Every time we had a burglary in the middle of the night, it seemed, the thieves were looking for those airplanes, since they were easy to sell illegally. And the ones we legitimately sold during the day came back to haunt us as well; every crash was "the airplane's fault." We couldn't call the customer a liar, so we'd have to refund the money.

We soon got out of that particular business.

In the late 1970s and early 1980s, the oil industry was booming in our home state of Oklahoma, where we had most of our stores at that time. Money was flowing freely; you could sell just about anything. We began adding quite expensive items such as luggage (people had money to travel), large grandfather clocks, ceiling fans, and art pieces that ran as high as $2,000 for signed and numbered lithographs. We put in a section of gourmet foods. We had classy miniature oil rigs in brass for up to $300, which companies would buy twenty and thirty at a time for their major investors. We opened a whole upstairs section above the main sales floor for this kind of merchandise.

We were getting off track, but we didn't know it. Then came the oil bust of 1985. Suddenly, discretionary money dried up. By the end of the year, we had lost $923,436—our first-ever year of red ink. In fact, that bottom-line loss was bigger than any two previous years of *profit*.

I still remember calling the family together in our living

room in April 1986. By then all three of our children, plus two nephews and our future son-in-law, were earning their living in the company. "I have some bad news, and I don't know what to do," I began. I explained that we were in serious trouble.

Our oldest son, Mart, then just twenty-four years old, said, "Dad, it's okay. Our faith is not in you—it's in God. If we lose the businesses, we'll still be okay."

> "DAD, IT'S OKAY. OUR FAITH IS NOT IN YOU—IT'S IN GOD. IF WE LOSE THE BUSINESSES, WE'LL STILL BE OKAY."

We talked about what we could do. We figured out where we had gone wrong. We clarified that we were first and foremost an arts-and-crafts store; those departments had to remain strong no matter what else beckoned for our attention. That was what most customers came to buy, even though they might pick up other items along the way.

As it turned out, the economy in our region rebounded fairly quickly. Within a few months, we began to see signs of profitability again. The year of 1986 ended in the black, and we've been able to stay there ever since. We believe God has helped us to make wise decisions, both in selecting merchandise and in other areas as well, in order to serve our customers and advance the company.

WELCOME TO OUR FOOTBALL FIELD

Today each Hobby Lobby store averages about 60,000 square feet—not exactly a "lobby," is it? It's more the size of a football field including both end zones. We opened our three-hundredth store in early 2003 and continue to open new ones about every two weeks from January through September. (Once the run-up to Christmas begins in October, we're too swamped to think about new stores.) Setting up a store has become a refined science; our teams can accomplish it in much faster time than it took us to restock that Tulsa store so long ago.

The first year we stocked for Christmas, we spent a whopping $2,000 on inventory. These days, we'll spend $220,000 *per store* on Christmas wreaths, ornaments, crafts, and everything else that makes the holiday so special.

> **THE FIRST YEAR WE STOCKED FOR CHRISTMAS, WE SPENT A WHOPPING $2,000 ON INVENTORY. THESE DAYS, WE'LL SPEND $220,000 PER STORE.**

Sometimes we sell more than we're aware of. A few years ago, a woman came into a Hobby Lobby and bought one of our large, unfinished ceramic pedestals to take home and paint for her yard. We had bought a forty-foot trailerload of them from Mexico, as I recall, where they had been cast and then set out in the warm sun to harden.

Because the pedestal was heavy, one of our teenage stock boys was assigned to help the lady get it out to her car. She opened the trunk, and as the young man tipped it sideways to fit it into the space . . . out of the pedestal's cavity came a live rattlesnake's head! It had apparently ridden there all the way from Mexico. Both the customer and the employee gasped and jumped back. Now what?!

Fortunately, the stock boy had the presence of mind to move the pedestal out of the trunk and quickly set it down on its base in the parking lot, with the snake still inside. He then ran inside to tell our manager, who called the city's animal control unit to come solve the problem.

Who knows how many days that snake had been silently resting on our showroom floor? Thankfully, no one had been bitten. As for the customer, you can be sure we checked the next pedestal thoroughly before taking it out to her car trunk.

When it comes to product selection, of course, there is such a thing as too many options. It can overwhelm the customer—and overwhelm our available space. We could offer two hundred kinds of silk roses if we wanted—but by stocking just fifteen varieties, we've found that we can get 95 percent of the available silk-rose business. It's up to each of our department buyers to listen to the customers and to what the stores are telling them, and make wise choices.

Buying is so very important. I don't want buyers who sit behind desks and stare at their computers; I want them out in the stores, in the real world, touching actual merchandise and seeing its appeal. We have eight merchandise managers, each with three to five buyers forming the team. Many of the buyers used to be secretaries, in fact. They don't have formal training, but they instinctively think like ordinary customers.

And they love what they do—going to trade shows, reading the trade magazines, hunting for fresh ideas wherever they can find them. Professional recruiters ("headhunters") are always trying to woo away our buyers for competitors, because they're so good at what they do. The headhunters almost never succeed.

When Hobby Lobby first began in 1972, arts and crafts were pretty much a ma-and-pa industry; retailers bought mostly from distributors and importers (middlemen). We had more latitude to make mistakes. Now, with competition sharpening and several large chains emerging, we have to be better at what we do.

I can't claim that we have dreamed up very many wonderful ideas from scratch. Most of the ideas come from a woman who starts doing a certain craft, and we try to serve her needs.

In our business, there's a difference between *fads* and *trends*. Fads come and go rapidly. Remember the battery-powered dancing flower a few years ago that would bob around in response to music or clapping your hands? That was a fad. You can lose a lot of money trying to chase these kinds of novelties.

Trends, on the other hand, rise slowly and decline slowly. In fact, over the past forty years, I've seen only four big trends in the world of crafts:

1. The 1970s: decoupage. People were taken with the idea of gluing prints to wood and then finishing them for display in their homes, on their purses, you name it.

2. The 1980s: macramé. We stocked tons of yarn in all kinds of colors and textures for this.

3. The 1990s: wearable art. People got excited about individualizing their sweatshirts, T-shirts, shoes, and other pieces of clothing with all manner of paints and appliqués.

4. Since the late 1990s: scrapbooking. We've enlarged from two side counters of scrapbook supplies up to twelve counters—not overnight,

but gradually as more product has become available and customer interest has grown. This trend has more staying power than the previous three, I predict, because it's not just about a certain style. It ties into people's deep values. They truly want to honor and remember the past.

All four of these came out of the blue, it seemed. Nobody predicted them, but they grew into huge departments.

Once a year, I give each buyer a sheet of paper with a line down the middle. The left side has a frowning face at the top, while the right has a smiley face. "On the left, please write down some product lines you think are waning," I instruct. "On the right, list some areas you think are coming on stronger these days." Naturally, everybody wants to hold on to all the space they have, but we must force ourselves to reevaluate and give space to the best categories and subcategories at the moment.

For example, wooden items from India are currently less popular than they used to be. The same is true of Indian brass (vases, candlesticks, planters) as well as candles and wicker baskets. Meanwhile, wall sconces are moving strongly; so are high-fashion yarns, ceramic tabletop items, and decorative garden items.

We're currently in the midst of the "Red Hat" surge—groups of women age fifty and up who get together mainly to have fun, laugh, and be a little outrageous now that their child-rearing duties are finished. Their inspiration comes from a poem by a British woman named Jenny Joseph, who wrote:

When I am an old woman, I shall wear purple
With a red hat which doesn't go, and doesn't suit me.

She then goes on to list all the outlandish things she wants to do.

They tell me that in these clubs, women under fifty aren't allowed to wear red and purple; instead, they have to wear pink hats and lavender outfits! Their statement of purpose on one Web site says, ". . . to greet middle age with verve, humor and élan. We believe silliness is the comedy relief of life."

Clearly, the demand for matching product is huge—everything from figurines to cards to ribbon to jewelry to napkins to candy in special wrappers. Obviously, we're paying attention; one of our female buyers has been assigned just to stay on track with the Red Hat phenomenon.

> ONE OF OUR FEMALE BUYERS HAS BEEN ASSIGNED JUST TO STAY ON TRACK WITH THE RED HAT PHENOMENON.

Whatever the product category, whether festive or functional, large or small, the goal across the Hobby Lobby store is to give the customer as much selection as is reasonable, making the whole experience a delight.

That's what I want to talk about in the next chapter: the shopping atmosphere.

CHAPTER 3

THE SHOPPING ATMOSPHERE

———— ⌒ ————

I freely admit that Hobby Lobby is not the spiffiest store on the American scene. We don't have carpet on the floor. There's no free food to sample—or even food to buy, like at the coffee bars in various bookstores these days. There's nobody in a tuxedo playing piano music in the atrium.

Instead, we're known for our value prices on do-it-yourself materials. We're very down-to-earth and practical.

But that doesn't mean we overlook the atmosphere for our shoppers. They may not arrive in chauffeured limousines, but they still want to enjoy the shopping experience.

Whatever the product line or type of store, I believe customers appreciate the following four things:

KEY 1: ORDERLINESS

At Hobby Lobby we're determined to keep a store that isn't junky—despite the nature of our merchandise. Crafts and home accents come in thousands of different shapes and sizes, which makes our job challenging. If we were in the clothing business, most items—whether men's, women's, or children's—would either display vertically on a hanger or stack nicely on a table. If we were car dealers, almost all vehicles would occupy roughly the same-size rectangles on the lot. We, on the other hand, are trying to keep an area that displays polyurethane grape clusters and dollhouse miniatures and ceramic birdbaths and model trains from looking like a junkyard.

I guess this is a personal fixation of mine. I've always been a "straightener-upper." In my high school years back in Altus, there were five of us kids plus my parents living in a two-bedroom house. (My older brother had already moved away by then.) So my parents got one bedroom, my three sisters got the other bedroom, and my brother and I made do with a rollaway in the kitchen. We had a little dresser there, and everything I owned went in just one drawer. There was no option for having stuff strewn all over the room. If you did, it would probably get swept into the garbage along with the breakfast banana peels before you knew it.

> MY PARENTS GOT ONE BEDROOM, MY THREE SISTERS GOT THE OTHER BEDROOM, AND MY BROTHER AND I MADE DO WITH A ROLLAWAY IN THE KITCHEN.

The teachers at school could tell our family wasn't exactly rich, probably by the clothes we wore. They were always clean, but certainly not expensive. Back in junior high in Mangum, Oklahoma, one of my teachers said to me one day, "You know, my husband is an electrician. He's

looking for a kid to hire, basically to be his gofer on the jobs.
Would you be at all interested in that?"

I jumped at the chance. Soon I was helping this man after
school and on Saturdays with his work. Not only did I run
back to the truck to get him various tools, but he also taught
me how to do simple installations such as wall sockets—
under his supervision, of course.

In between jobs, it didn't take me long to notice that his
shop back home was a total disaster. He had switches in
eight or ten different places, for example. If he or I were
looking for something, it would take quite a while to poke
through all the different places it might be.

I saw this as an exciting challenge. On my own, I started
organizing the place. I sorted tools into one location and all
the various kinds of parts into similar categories. The more
orderly the shop became, the prouder I was.

The man walked in one day and said, "Hey, this is pretty
good! Thanks, David."

My teacher added one day at school, "Wow—you really
surprised my husband. He had no idea the shop could look
so good."

My next job during high school was at McClellan's. I've
already mentioned how I set to work organizing the glass
and fixture room.

When I quit McClellan's to work for TG&Y, my first
job was as an assistant manager in Shawnee, Oklahoma. I
was only twenty years old. The manager, I could tell, was
not especially happy about headquarters sending him what
he assumed was a young rookie, so he decided to try to
break me. He dispatched me to the store basement, which
was a mess.

There, within a couple of weeks, the stockroom was

transformed. All the fixtures were together, the stock was in organized bins, and you could actually find what you were looking for. He came downstairs one day, and his only comment was "Ya know, we're not slave drivers around here. It's okay for you to take a break."

Cleaning up and staying organized has become a lifelong habit for me. My son Steve, who is now Hobby Lobby's president, teases me about being a "neat freak." My idea of fun on a Saturday afternoon is to go out to some property I have and clean out the underbrush. Turning a tangled mass of foliage into an attractive area of trees that I can actually walk through puts a smile on my face.

> MY SON STEVE TEASES ME ABOUT BEING A "NEAT FREAK." MY IDEA OF FUN ON A SATURDAY AFTERNOON IS TO GO OUT TO SOME PROPERTY I HAVE AND CLEAN OUT THE UNDERBRUSH.

During the rest of the week, I insist that Hobby Lobby should be well organized—not just because it's my nature, but because customers appreciate it. They like being able to find what they're seeking with a minimum of looking around.

Of all our departments, I suppose Halloween is the hardest to keep straight. That's because a lot of kids come shopping in that department, so it's very difficult. (Over the last few years, we've been stocking less Halloween stuff and more items along the themes of harvest, autumn, and Thanksgiving. Some people who object to Halloween complain that we carry any of that merchandise at all. There's a lot that we rule out on the grounds that it's just too ghoulish and bloody. We have elected, however, to take a middle road here, and we don't feel guilty about the things we do stock.)

Another department that can get messy very quickly is hobbies—again, because of the children traffic. Don't get me wrong: I love kids and love them coming to Hobby Lobby. Most of them aren't trying to create disaster; they're just inquisitive little folks who want to see and touch things. So we have to work harder at keeping the department attractive for the next customer after they leave.

Home accents is a third area of challenge, because tens of thousands of items come in all kinds of sizes and shapes. We try to group them by theme or color.

The fact that we don't use bar coding on our merchandise (a subject I'll address more fully in chapter 6) means the staff members have no computer list to indicate what they should reorder. Instead, they have to go to the aisle and actually *look* at the merchandise, taking note of what's below minimum level. This has a way of making our people keep their departments straightened up! Otherwise, they won't know what to reorder.

"Auto-replacement"—the business term for letting the computer decide what to order—sounds like a good idea. But if merchandise just automatically arrives at the back door because some computer said so, it can easily be thrown onto a counter or a wall rack without the careful thought it deserves.

Orderliness in the store is subjective, in a way, just as it is in your home or mine. How orderly is "good enough"? Years ago, we came up with some criteria for district managers to use in evaluating a given store. How straight is the merchandise? Are there any empty bins? Have items returned by customers been put back in place, or are they still sitting in a pile somewhere? Are there any burned-out lightbulbs? Are the floors clean and waxed? Is there dust under any of the pushcarts? Are the windows clean? What about the restrooms?

Each month the district manager walks through each of his or her twenty or so stores taking note of these things. Eventually it comes down to a rating. This isn't a mathematical formula; it's more of a judgment call, like an English teacher grading an essay. But the result is very definite: Any rating of less than 90 percent means this particular store manager needs help.

We also have a standing policy that the last thirty to sixty minutes of the evening is what we call "recovery time." Before everybody goes home, they need to straighten items, pull stock to the front of the shelves, and put returns back where they belong. That way, when people come in the next morning, the store looks its best.

> THERE'S NO QUESTION IN MY MIND
> THAT WE CANNOT BE THE BEST
> IN OUR FIELD IF WE'RE SLOPPY AT
> ANYTHING WE DO.

Behind the scenes, it's the same story. Our back offices, filing systems, break rooms, conference rooms—they all need to look sharp. There's no question in my mind that we cannot be the best in our field if we're sloppy at anything we do.

People may say this costs extra money. I say it actually costs *more* in wages if we're disorganized. Regular tasks in a store take longer if you're messy. On the other hand, if things are in good order, the work moves along briskly.

KEY 2: SPACIOUSNESS

The atmosphere of Hobby Lobby is supposed to provide room enough to breathe. The aisles are wide enough to maneuver, and the island displays aren't crammed together.

This is a gift to the customers. From our point of view, we'd be more profitable if we "racked-and-stacked" things higher, jamming the available square footage. Business analysts sometimes evaluate retail operations on the basis of "sales per square foot," and by that standard we're not the top dog. But we think that indirectly, our spaciousness comes back to pay us dividends by giving the customer a more pleasant experience.

Mothers sometimes tell us, "I was over at one of your competitors with my child in a shopping cart, and even if I was right in the center of the aisle, he was still able to grab stuff from both sides. I hate that!"

Even shoppers without children appreciate being able to get around someone who has stopped to browse in an aisle without having to say, "Excuse me—may I get past you?"

As we've added new departments over the years, it has forced us to lease bigger facilities. Some of our older stores, frankly, are too crowded. About forty-five of them are on a list to be expanded or relocated.

We rate locations on a scale from 1 to 10, a 10 being directly across the street from a large mall with major anchor stores. Yet the price to lease such a prime location can be over the top as far as Hobby Lobby is concerned. The landlord might earn a profit, but we wouldn't.

So no matter the prestige, we'll go a half mile down the road to an 8 or 9 location to get the required space at the right price. We'll give up a little prestige to maintain the size the customer will enjoy. We know, of course, that to some extent, we're a "destination store"—people come to shop with us intentionally, regardless of our address.

About 80 percent of our locations are second-generation. In other words, the building used to be, say, a Wal-Mart that moved out to become a Super Wal-Mart, or a Kmart that closed. It seems such a site becomes available almost every year in every city. The economics of these sites are usually better than building from the ground up.

In this way we provide the spaciousness that our customers like, without breaking the bank.

KEY 3: HELPFULNESS

Every retailer claims to have a helpful workforce, I know. Whether the public agrees is sometimes another story.

EVERY RETAILER CLAIMS TO HAVE A HELPFUL WORKFORCE, I KNOW. WHETHER THE PUBLIC AGREES IS SOMETIMES ANOTHER STORY.

The average sale in a Hobby Lobby is no more than $20. Obviously, that dictates how much help any customer can receive. We simply cannot afford to hold the hand of each customer the way a stockbroker or a real estate agent would, where the profit is hundreds of times greater.

But that doesn't mean we dismiss the idea of greeting customers, being friendly, and staying pleasant. Every question deserves an answer. Whenever we hear, "Where is such-and-such?" our people normally escort the customer to the precise aisle rather than just pointing "over there somewhere."

I was pleased to hear the story of one man who was sent by his wife to get some floating candles. Rather than hunt around, he walked up to a woman in her late thirties wearing a blue Hobby Lobby vest who was pricing candy near the front of the store.

"Where would I find those little floating candles?" he asked.

By the woman's hand motions, the customer realized almost immediately that she was speech-and-hearing impaired. She had not heard his question, and she could not speak back to him. But before he could walk away or even feel embarrassed, she had whipped out of her pocket a pen and a small pad of paper. She extended it to the man with a hopeful expression on her face.

He took the pad and scribbled "floating candles?" then handed it back.

Her face instantly brightened as she motioned for the man to follow her. Across the store they trekked, arriving at the candle aisle. She specifically pointed him to the shelf where the floating varieties lay.

He smiled and nodded, saying, "Thank you!" even though she couldn't hear him. And with that, she disappeared back to her candy cart.

The man told me later, "I was struck by two things. Number one, that Hobby Lobby was even willing to hire such a person for a retail, meet-the-public kind of job. And number two, that she was totally prepared to answer customer questions. She had thought it all out in advance that she would no doubt be approached by customers, and so she must think of a way to dialogue with them. I was impressed!"

Generally speaking, Hobby Lobby is a self-service operation. One major exception, however, is our framing department. We have to work with the customer to pick the right molding, the right mat, and glass for their piece of art, certificate, poster, or photo. And we think we have some very good people across the chain who do this.

Way back in the beginning at our second store on Tenth Street in Oklahoma City, we developed a framing table not in the back room but right out on the sales floor, where customers could watch what was going on. All the glass, cardboard backing, dustcover material, hangers, and everything else required were right there. All the tools were near at hand. We still do that today. It enables customers to make sure the finished product is going to please them, and to walk out with their fully framed picture in a matter of minutes.

On a busy Saturday, you'll see as many as four employees working at the table, one on each corner. This is unique to us; it's been a great benefit to our customers to not have to come back later for their cherished picture. If it fits in a standard-size frame, they can take it home right away.

As you might expect, this department has the highest wage cost of any in the store. But we price the service accordingly so that it pays its way, and people appreciate what they get.

Being helpful to the customer can occasionally go to extremes, we've found. One day in our Denver store on

Monaco Parkway, a very pregnant woman stopped in to pick up her mother. While standing on the sales floor, her water broke.

The staff came to her aid right away and ushered her back to a classroom, while somebody quickly dialed 911. They eased the woman up onto a table and held her hand, waiting for the paramedics to arrive.

Well, as it turned out, this baby was in no mood to wait for an ambulance ride to the hospital. It was born right there in Hobby Lobby. I'm glad to report that everything worked out fine.

> THIS BABY WAS IN NO MOOD TO WAIT
> FOR AN AMBULANCE RIDE TO THE
> HOSPITAL. IT WAS BORN RIGHT THERE
> IN HOBBY LOBBY.

In retail, you never quite know what's going to be asked of you.

KEY 4: AMBIENCE

A less specific attribute of a store is its overall ambience. Something about our pace and environment creates a sense of peace. As a result, we hear people talking about Hobby Lobby time as their "escape" or their "reward," almost as if we were some kind of haven in a frenetic world. I even heard about one little four-year-old girl who, while riding in her car seat, would often ask, "Mommy, can we go to Hobby Lobby?"

"Why would you want to do that?" the mother would inquire. It wasn't as if we had a flashy toy department.

"I just like it when we go there," was the girl's only explanation.

Part of the ambience is certainly our choice of music. We've contracted with the Muzak Corporation to create what they call a Satellite Signature channel exclusively for us. We've told them we want a mix of instrumental music that is uplifting but not harsh, something that enhances the atmosphere without dominating or distracting.

The repertoire is a combination of classical and inspirational music, chosen by one of Muzak's programmers who submits a daily playlist to our head office for review. We constantly move music in and out of the playlist depending on what we feel is appropriate and of high quality.

Customers who are Christians usually recognize selections they've heard in their churches or at a concert, and they express their appreciation. Other shoppers don't pay conscious attention to the music, but still they sense its soothing touch. We get a lot of letters and e-mails about the music. Someone feeling down might walk into the store, for example, and say, "You turned my whole spirit around by the music you played that day."

Another part of ambience is lighting. When preparing a second-generation site, we usually completely redo the fixtures. It's important to us to have a well-lighted store.

Once an elderly man came into a Hobby Lobby and commented, "I've never in my life seen so much stuff that no one needs!" Well, in a sense he was right; you don't *have* to have anything that Hobby Lobby sells. That is actually a positive; instead of feeling driven, customers can relax and enjoy the experience. It's different from going to the grocery store or stopping at the mass merchandiser for diapers.

A lot of our managers, in fact, come from such environments. They frequently tell us, "You know, here it's very different from where I used to work. The customer is in a different mood. It's not so intense."

We're trying to embellish that fact as much as we can. We want people to enjoy their purchasing, even if, technically speaking, they don't *have* to have that beaded lampshade or that pair of wall sconces.

> WE WANT PEOPLE TO ENJOY THEIR
> PURCHASING, EVEN IF, TECHNICALLY
> SPEAKING, THEY DON'T HAVE TO HAVE
> THAT BEADED LAMPSHADE OR THAT
> PAIR OF WALL SCONCES.

This makes life more pleasant for our employees, by the way. When customers are having a good time, it's easier for the staff to have a good time as well.

CHAPTER 4

90 PERCENT OFF?!

Everybody loves a bargain. The joy of paying less for something than your neighbor paid last week is delicious. It confers bragging rights: "Boy, did I get a deal on this Christmas tree (or refrigerator, or airfare, or condominium)! I saved so much money you wouldn't believe it."

That's why our company logo is a circle with two bold claims emblazoned above and below a middle banner that says "Everyday!" The bottom half of the circle says "Super Selection," a topic I addressed in chapter 2. The top half proclaims "Super Savings." Those are our two claims to fame.

Every Sunday in the newspaper of every city where we operate, a Hobby Lobby ad will tell you what's on sale that week. "All Brass Items—30% Off! All Silk Flowers—40% Off!" Our customers get into a rhythm of checking the Sunday paper to see which are the good deals for the next six days.

I'm thankful to be functioning in an economic climate here in America that allows me this kind of flexibility. I would hate to be retailing in some of the European countries

where there are rigid price laws. For example, if a book publisher determines that a certain book is to be sold for 15
euros, that's it—you dare not offer it for 12.95 euros. The
police would be knocking on your office door.

On the other hand, I've walked through the open-air
markets of some Asian or Latin American countries where
every price is negotiable. You are expected to haggle over the
smallest item. This certainly makes for a lively marketplace,
although shopping takes a lot longer. I can't imagine what it
would be like if every woman coming into Hobby Lobby
wanted to argue over the price of a knitting needle; we'd
never get the checkout line moving.

> ## THE AVERAGE WOMAN WILL PAY
> ## AS MUCH AS $1,353 EXTRA TO AVOID
> ## NEGOTIATING THE PRICE OF A CAR.

A curious book came out recently asserting that men
view all this differently from women. According to Carnegie
Mellon economist Linda Babcock and Sara Laschever in
Women Don't Ask: Negotiation and the Gender Divide,[1] a
survey asked men to pick a good metaphor for negotiation.
Their answer: "winning a ball game." Women, on the other
hand, were asked the same question and picked "going to
the dentist." For a lot of men, apparently, price haggling is a
sport, a chance to show you can beat the other guy, which is
something they enjoy. The average woman, meanwhile, will
pay as much as $1,353 extra to avoid negotiating the price
of a car, claim the authors.

Of course there are exceptions to the above—in both

directions. But going along with the general rule, we don't make Hobby Lobby shoppers (the majority of whom are women) haggle over our prices. Instead, we offer sales, which are an automatic delight.

THE STARTING POINT

Sales, of course, are based on a discount from the standard price, which is something we try to set reasonably in the first place. A Kansas City radio station recently did a comparison survey of twenty items between Hobby Lobby and a home-and-craft competitor. They announced that, on average, Hobby Lobby was 12 percent lower than the other store. I was glad to hear that, of course; that's the way I want things to be all the time.

Customers may wonder just how we decide the price of an item. The truth is, with 100,000 items to handle, we can't spend a lot of time agonizing over each glitter package or piece of matboard. Instead, we give each of our buyers a margin target for their department. "Margin" is the accounting term for the difference between what an item costs coming in the back door and what we collect when it goes out the front door. In between those two numbers is the money it takes to cover the operation—everything from wages to rent to utilities to breakage to shoplifting. As long as a buyer meets the overall margin required for his or her department, I'm happy.

There's another factor, however—the state of the competition in a particular location. Any Hobby Lobby manager anywhere is authorized to cut prices to match the local competitor. If we in the home office in Oklahoma City say that a set of Christmas lights should be priced at $1.77, but a mass merchandiser in Chicago offers it for $1.57, our local manager should instantly cut the price to $1.57.

ANY HOBBY LOBBY MANAGER ANYWHERE IS AUTHORIZED TO CUT PRICES TO MATCH THE LOCAL COMPETITOR.

At the time of this writing, Red Heart yarn is selling at Wal-Mart for $1.17 a skein. Considering the cost of doing business these days, I could not break even at that price—but I absolutely refuse to have customers think they can buy yarn cheaper at Wal-Mart than Hobby Lobby. So our price is $1.17. We'll make our profits on something else. (Fortunately, we don't have to compete head-to-head with Wal-Mart on very many items!)

I've made my share of pricing mistakes over the years, of course. The biggest one was the time a needlework distributor was going out of business and sold us two or three truckloads of kits at a ridiculous price—somewhere between $1.00 and $1.50 apiece. We marked them up to the $2–3 range and put them out for sale.

Well, the customers just went crazy, of course. What a bargain this was for them. The only problem was, I had no way to continue at this price level. Once the closeout kits were gone, we were back to the normal price of $16, and the whole needlework department went dead for a while.

Value in the retail business is the proper combination of two things: quality and price. You can have extremely high quality—a hand-carved walnut picture frame, for example—

but if it costs $100, it's not an acceptable value to the customer. At the other extreme, you could slap some boards together and offer a picture frame for $1.29 that would fall apart the first time the customer tried to mount something; that wouldn't be a good value, either.

We tell our buyers, "Never let this single focus get away from you: finding good value for the customer. A useful product for an attractive price—that's what you're looking for."

THE DISCOUNT DANCE

Having set a foundation of reasonable prices, we then come to the "sale!" mind-set that I outlined at the beginning of this chapter. Even if the standard price is reasonable, people still love to get it cheaper.

And sometimes I, as a merchant, have reason to agree with them. Seasonal items, for example, need to be cleared from the store as soon as the holiday is over, no matter what it takes. Starting on December 26, all our Christmas merchandise goes 50 percent off. A few days later, we go to two-thirds off. A few days after that, we cut to 80 percent off. Finally, we hit 90 percent off—and within a day or two, the shelves are bare.

Am I losing money on the 90 percent blowout? Of course I am. But not nearly as much as I'd be losing if I had to haul that Christmas stuff back to some warehouse, put it away, sit on it for ten months paying storage expenses, and then drag it back out to the stores for Christmastime next year. Plus, the customers would have already seen it last year. I'm better off getting rid of it.

Even if one of our buyers mistakenly bought too much

stock for the season, I'd rather move it out at a loss so we can start next time with a clean slate.

Obviously, we couldn't afford to sell those items at 90 percent off all through the Christmas season. But when we put the whole effort together on one spreadsheet, from the beginning until the last item is gone in early January, the numbers work out after all.

By the way, people sometimes wonder why we display Christmas items so early—some of them as early as June. "Aren't you kind of rushing things?" they'll say. "We haven't even had Thanksgiving yet!"

What they don't know is that the serious craftspeople are pushing us from the other side, saying, "Hey, I've got to be ready for two craft shows in September, and I need time to make my stuff. Where's your Christmas ribbon? Where are those floral picks you always carry every year?"

Some of our sales have nothing at all to do with holidays. Twice a year, we go through the product list and simply clean house. Every one of the "push" items (those that we send out on a onetime basis) has a date code on its price tag. Right after Mother's Day and then again after Christmas, we go through the store and pick up everything that has been sitting for a certain length of time. Off the items go to the sale tables, where we start slashing prices to get rid of them. This keeps the store looking clean and fresh.

A store manager or department head can't afford to be sentimental at this moment. "Oh, but I really like this cute figurine—we ought to keep it on hand a little while longer." If a customer hasn't bought it in its designated window of time, I'm sorry—it's outta there. As I often say, "I'd rather have a dollar in the cash register than two dollars sitting on the shelf."

If you never clean out slow-moving stock, you eventually strangle yourself. Your store gets logjammed with no place to put new items that the customers will find interesting, and no cash to buy them with. Your business will be stagnant.

> **IF YOU NEVER CLEAN OUT SLOW-MOVING STOCK, YOU EVENTUALLY STRANGLE YOURSELF.**

All of our store managers know that the flow of new, fresh merchandise is *not* going to stop. Those trucks are going to keep rolling in from Oklahoma City every week, so they might as well get ready for them by cleaning out the slow merchandise.

And so . . . another sale is born.

THE FOREIGN FACTOR

Part of the reason our margins allow us to have sales is that a fair number of our products come from East Asia. This is a controversial topic, I realize. American newspapers and politicians are talking a lot these days about the job drain. You might walk through the aisles of Hobby Lobby and accuse us of making matters worse by importing so much from overseas.

I don't deny that this is a serious matter. When any American loses a job to offshore competition, that person and his family suffer deeply. The unemployment line is an awful place to be. And, among other things, those without a job won't be spending money at Hobby Lobby very often.

I do have some observations to make about the foreign factor, however.

First of all, in our line of business, a large portion of our items are simply not available from a North American source. I can't offer you a wide selection of competitively priced florals, for example, without going overseas. Where do people sit and attach silk petals to a stem one at a time, hour after hour? China. If you want nice-looking, artificial flowers for your dining room table, there's not much choice.

Decorative baskets are another such item. More than 90 percent of these come from the Philippines, Indonesia, and China. Actually, I did find one domestic source for baskets— and I would have had to price them at $80 apiece!

Red Heart yarn, which I mentioned earlier, is an American brand, and we are proud to carry it. But there are also some very beautiful yarns that we can get only in such places as Turkey, Taiwan, and Italy.

A fourth example would be Christmas ornaments. I can't run a Christmas department without the vast array of decorations that come from Asia. It is a simple matter of what people in that part of the world are willing to work for versus what Americans are willing to pay. Which do you want: our American minimum-wage law of $5.15 an hour, or hand-painted Christmas ornaments for $1.99 each? You can't have both.

I often say to people that I don't make the nation's trading laws; I just obey them. If Congress wants to rule that American companies stop importing goods from East Asia, I'll halt all orders the first thing tomorrow morning. I'll close our two buying offices in Hong Kong and Manila. I'll stop our buying trips to as many as thirty countries overseas.

Whatever the U.S. government decides is best for the economy will get my cooperation.

But the aftermath of such a ruling would be dramatic. A
lot of popular items on the Hobby Lobby shelves would dis-
appear. And the prices of other items would balloon to
shocking levels. The American consumer would be in for a
rude awakening.

Furthermore, a fair number of *American* jobs would be
affected. The longshoremen at the Port of Los Angeles who
unload our incoming containers from the ships, for example,
and the crews on the Union Pacific Railroad who haul those
containers from L.A. to Dallas, where our trucks pick them
up and bring them north to Oklahoma City, could all lose
their jobs. We're unloading an average of 50 shipping containers the size of a boxcar each working day, or 12,000 a
year. All of that would undergo huge disruption.

Nearly everything we buy overseas, by the way, draws a
duty assessment. On some candles we pay as high as 95 percent extra. On a lot of glassware, we pay an additional 30
percent. These are all set by U.S. Customs to tilt the playing
field in favor of American manufacturers.

> WE'RE UNLOADING AN AVERAGE
> OF 50 SHIPPING CONTAINERS THE SIZE
> OF A BOXCAR EACH WORKING DAY,
> OR 12,000 A YEAR.

The government could double or triple these duty rates,
I suppose. However, the reaction of foreign countries who
import from us going the other direction would be to

retaliate. This would make it tougher for Microsoft, Motorola, Gillette, and others trying to sell abroad. As I say, it's a complicated matter.

Aside from duties, we who import have the unavoidable burden of shipping across the ocean. If you've ever flown to Tokyo, Hong Kong, Singapore, you know that the Pacific is a very wide obstacle! Our rule of thumb is that it costs us $2 per cubic foot to bring something in from overseas. This, unavoidably, gets built into the prices we charge customers.

That is why flat or compact things usually make better economic sense to import than big, bulky things. Take our unfinished wood furniture—end tables or shelving—as one example. We could buy it from a North American source and truck it to our warehouse. Or we could buy it far cheaper from a Chinese source, but its bulkiness would erase much of the advantage en route. The third option turns out to be the best for the customer: We buy the individual wood pieces *flat* from the Chinese source, then assemble them in our 750,000-square-foot manufacturing building in Oklahoma City.

The crazy part is that the Chinese don't even grow a lot of their own wood in the first place! They buy much of it on the lumber market in the United States and Canada, haul it west across the ocean, cut it up to furniture specifications, sometimes add wonderful hand-carving, then ship it back east to our country again—and still beat everybody else's price. Go figure.

We used to sew all our own T-shirts and sweatshirts for our section of wearable art. I was buying the material from American mills and hiring more than 120 people to make the garments. I thought everything was fine.

Then came the day when a salesman from Hanes (or perhaps Fruit of the Loom) walked in our front door offering to supply us with T-shirts and sweatshirts of equal quality that were being sewn in Haiti for less than I could do it myself in our own plant. They had been sewing their goods in the United States the last time I checked—but this was a wake-up call. I had a choice to make: I could either go offshore as they had done, or get out of the business altogether. Competition forces you to make hard decisions.

I decided to go offshore. To this day, we still buy the cloth from American mills. But we ship it to the Caribbean for sewing at a per-piece rate, then ship it back here to sell.

Along the way, I had to worry about what to do with my 120 employees. I stewed around for an extra year under the old system, not wanting to lay anybody off. I finally realized we could redeploy these people from clothing to making throw pillows, which is what we do today. Pillow-making is here to stay, I believe, because it requires so many elements from so many different countries. Some of our pillows are a composite of materials from five different nations! The top may come from Italy, the bottom from the United States, the fiberfill insert from Korea, the tassel from Mexico, and the fringe from China. We think we do a better job on throw pillows than anybody else in terms of design as well as price. And nobody on our payroll lost their job.

LOTS TO THINK ABOUT

The global economy is forcing all of us to consider difficult questions. I find it interesting to notice that many of my critics will complain about our carrying Chinese vases while at the same time they think nothing of driving a Toyota or a

Volvo, talking on a Nokia cell phone (Finland), taking flights on an Airbus 320 (assembled in France) instead of a Boeing 737—and even carrying a Bible that was printed in Holland, Belgium, or South Korea. Those in the Bible publishing field have told me that their sources are limited to printers that can handle the thin paper required for Bibles. And one of the most economical is a mission printing company in Minsk, Belarus. Why are its prices so good? Because people in Belarus (next door to Russia) are willing to work for $1.75 an hour, whereas the average hourly wage in U.S. printing plants is around $17–18 an hour.

Is it wrong for churches and mission groups to save scarce money by printing Bibles in Belarus? Or is that good stewardship?

> CHINA VERY MUCH WANTS THE BUSINESS OF AMERICAN RETAILERS. THEY'LL DO A LOT TO PLEASE US—WHICH OPENS THE DOOR FOR DISCUSSION ABOUT HUMANITARIAN CONCERNS.

Belarus, by the way, currently has a very repressive government; it hasn't made a great deal of progress since the old Communist days. The same is true of China; I am well aware of how the Beijing government pressures the Christian churches, especially those that are unregistered. Some would say we should have no business dealings whatsoever as a result.

On the other hand, China very much wants the business of American retailers. They'll do a lot to please us—

which opens the door for discussion about humanitarian concerns.

Furthermore, one has to remember that the individual employee in a printing plant or a craft factory who is trying to feed his family is not the same as the atheistic government that dominates him. All God's children need an income—American, Canadian, Chinese, Indonesian, whomever. Barbara and I still remember the little Filipino lady who broke down in tears when we gave an order for two containers of baskets to her consortium of home workers. "You don't know how much this means to us," she cried. "Now two hundred families will be able to support themselves."

Those baskets wound up on the tables and fireplace mantels of folks in Colorado, Indiana, and Alabama at a price they could afford. The customer was pleased, and the suppliers back in the Philippines were ecstatic. This is what happens in retail every day. If there is a fairer way to make this happen, I'm willing to listen. In the meantime, Hobby Lobby will keep searching for the best methods and systems to bring our customers great products.

And we'll even put them on sale.

PART TWO

BEHIND
THE SCENES

CHAPTER 5

THREE WAYS TO GUARD THE BOTTOM LINE

It's one thing to make a lot of sales. It's quite another to manage a retail company in such a way as to preserve the benefit of those sales. In other words, it does no good to bring in $1 million if you spend $1.1 million along the way. The top line on your financial report may look impressive, but the bottom line will let the air out of your enthusiasm as well as your banker's.

Every year the business section of the newspaper reports billion-dollar companies falling by the wayside. Their deterioration didn't happen overnight. Instead, for years too many people, from the executive suite on down, focused on their internal needs (corporate and personal) instead of the customers' needs. Any expense a company incurs eventually has to be paid by the customers, anyway. If we don't buy product at the right price, if our operating expenses are too high, the customer will eventually vote no on our viability.

We need to have a clear vision of whom we're working for. Our loyalties in the long run are not to a salesman who needs a commission, or to a vendor who wants to get rich quick. It is to the customer. If we lose sight of this, the numbers won't work for us.

J. C. Penney once made a curious statement: "I am unselfish for selfish reasons." What he meant was that he would do everything he could to bring the customer the very best products at the best price . . . so that eventually he would make a profit.

I believe in paying constant attention to the costs of doing business. Sales dollars can seep away in three main areas. Each of these requires vigilant defense against the thousand-and-one little nibbles that erode profitability.

CHECKPOINT 1: THE COST OF PRODUCT

The wisdom of getting quality product at the lowest possible cost should be obvious to everyone. But it is not something you can accomplish with a dramatic move once a year and then forget about it. I find I have to keep digging at it every day.

If Hobby Lobby is not buying something directly from the factory where it is made, I immediately get suspicious. We're paying some middleman somewhere—and middlemen don't work for free. When we first began importing a lot of goods from Asia, it was far easier to work with trading companies and importers. They could speak the language of the manufacturers overseas, do all the paperwork for shipping, and so forth. But this service came at a price.

Today, whenever we can deal directly with the factory, we do. We keep our product costs as low as possible, so we can stay competitive in the marketplace.

I ask our buyers to show me the savings gained in their

purchasing this year compared to last. I'm expecting them to always work for a better price on each item without compromising quality. At a certain time of year, each of the buyers presents his or her numbers: "Last year, I paid this much for tea lights, but this year I got them for this much cheaper." We appreciate this—and reward their efforts with a bonus.

We will even push to get the factory to package its product the way we want it—and 99 percent of the time, it'll do it. The Asians are especially cooperative in this regard. We tell them how big to make the packaging, what it should say in English, what colors it should use—and they follow through. Some of the other nationalities aren't quite as adept at this, but we insist. Otherwise, we bring the product back to the United States in bulk and do the packaging ourselves.

If a supplier's costs aren't working out on a given product we want to carry, we don't hesitate to figure out how to make it cheaper ourselves. In the previous chapter, I mentioned our manufacturing building in Oklahoma City. It's the strangest hodgepodge of operations you ever saw—everything from pillows to furniture to candles to picture frames to scented potpourri, all under one roof. In every case, we are making the item to reduce the cost of product.

The frame department is cranking out 6,000 to 10,000 frames a day to be sold across the Hobby Lobby chain. One-fourth of these are the rough "barnwood" style that is so popular. In addition, the same department is making another 2,500 custom frames a day for customers who want to mount an odd size. Stores take the orders, letting the customers choose among 320 different styles of molding, and send the information to headquarters once a week. We make the frames to fit and send them to the stores.

In another room, people are stretching and stapling canvas onto frames for those who like to paint. This is a standard line of any art store. I realized a few years ago that we could save the cost of a shipping box if we would stack the frames in groups of six, bundle them with the "good" side facing inward for protection, and staple them together tightly across the edges using leftover scraps of canvas that were going to be thrown out anyway. This single maneuver saves us around $200,000 a year.

It's amazing how, on large volumes of product, one modest idea can add up to a lot of money over time.

When other kinds of products do require a shipping carton, we use it—but we insist on recycling. The sides are clearly marked: "Break down and return to warehouse." No sense throwing cartons away at the store level, which just costs money to replace—and swells the local landfills.

> WHEN PRODUCTS REQUIRE A SHIPPING CARTON, WE USE THEM—BUT WE INSIST ON RECYCLING. THE SIDES ARE CLEARLY MARKED: "BREAK DOWN AND RETURN TO WAREHOUSE."

We used to buy matboard from one of the two American sources. Eventually we discovered we could make it cheaper ourselves.

We also manufacture huge numbers of rubber stamps for the scrapbooking crowd. We hold the exclusive stamp license for all the *Peanuts* characters, for example. That means our main competitor buys from us if they want Charlie Brown or Snoopy stamps.

In the next room of our plant, people are assembling potpourri from elements gathered in India and elsewhere. We have to do this ourselves, because the fragrance has a shelf life; it weakens over time.

Most of the candles we sell (about $12 million worth every year) are made in our factory instead of purchased from vendors—even though I tease our people by pretending to "hate" this operation. Why? Because it's so messy! The wax gets all over everything; the vats smell . . . it's just not my favorite atmosphere. But they know I'm kidding, and that it makes good economic sense for us to be candlemakers. The crew, in fact, does a wonderful job.

Creative Leisure News, a trade publication in our field, once ran an article on what makes Hobby Lobby successful and interviewed a number of our vendors. One marketing vice president answered, "They may have the lowest product costs in the industry because they manufacture so much themselves and import a much larger proportion of products directly from Asia than any other craft retailer." (The key word there is *directly*. Our competitors probably buy as high a percentage of their stock from Asia as we do, but we tend to go directly to the factories for ours, thus getting a better price.)

Another manufacturer who has sold to us for close to ten years said, "They do straightforward business, take a chance on something new, and give purchase orders up front to match their capacity. It is one of my most enjoyable accounts to work with; the buyer cares, is receptive, and responsive. If you do the same unto them, you win."

This kind of comment shows that we are quite willing to

take products from outside sources as well as to make them ourselves. It just depends on the numbers. Either way, we are determined to spend no more than necessary.

CHECKPOINT 2: STORE EXPENSES

As you might imagine, it's quite a trick to sit in Oklahoma City and control what is being spent every day by store managers in Terre Haute, Indiana; Baton Rouge, Louisiana; and Rapid City, South Dakota. But this is another vital checkpoint in the managing of costs.

The biggest single item for us is total payroll. How much should a store be allowed to spend on people?

We recognize that wage scales vary from place to place, and so we don't try to set them nationally. We allow the store managers to determine local pay and give out raises as they see fit. Our control mechanism works like this: "Hire as many staff as you want, and pay as much as you want—up to 11 percent of your gross sales." In other words, if you are a $3 million store, you can spend up to $330,000 a year on payroll—including yourself.

WE ALLOW THE STORE MANAGERS TO DETERMINE LOCAL PAY AND GIVE OUT RAISES AS THEY SEE FIT.

I view a store's employees sort of like a football team, with the store manager as the coach. He or she is the one who recruits, trains, motivates, organizes—and ought to be able to win games with eleven players. If you don't have the right players to make it work, then maybe you need to trade. This is an oversimplified analogy, of course, but it illustrates the point. We have stores all over the country doing very well on 11 percent. It's mainly a matter of good coaching.

The only variable, and it's a fairly minor one, is store sales volume. A high-volume store can get by on 10 or even 9 percent for payroll, whereas a low-volume store may need 12 or 13 percent. But the average allowance is 11 percent, and it works well.

Someone may protest, "Well, wages in Chicago are higher than in, say, Dodge City, Kansas, so your system isn't fair." I grant that retail wages may be higher—but in such an area of the country, everybody else's wages are higher too. This means customers have more dollars in their pockets and thus do more spending. Therefore, store income should be higher as well. The 11 percent wage budget remains a pretty good rule of thumb.

I cannot emphasize strongly enough that success in retail is the result of building a strong staff—and a manager can't do this without paying people fairly. Tenure is only one part of the decision; an even more important factor in setting wages is productivity. If two or three employees are not being productive, the manager is going to have to hire extra people to pick up the slack—and that's going to ruin the wage budget. If the manager tries to keep a lid on things by holding back on raises for the true producers, that will just dishearten and irritate them, causing further loss in productivity. The whole atmosphere in the store will deteriorate.

It is far better to deal with the problem people, even replacing them if need be, in order to keep the whole team on the winning side.

From the manager's point of view, we use a quarterly

bonus system. We control overspending on payroll by saying to store managers that if they hit their 11 percent target, they'll get a nice extra at the end of three months. If they come in at 11.1 percent, they forfeit a tenth of the bonus. If they come in at 11.2 percent, they forfeit two-tenths of the bonus. If their wages get all the way up to 12 percent, they've lost it all.

We don't have to nag or scold; we let the store manager's spouse take care of that!

"Honey, what happened to your bonus this quarter? I was really looking forward to buying that new sofa."

"Uh, well, I kind of let my payroll costs get out of hand . . ."

After all, payroll expense is not from the manager's personal funds; he or she is spending the company's money here. Any manager who goes overboard needs to feel the pain—and on a prompt schedule. Once a year isn't often enough for a category this large; it needs to be quarterly.

> ## ANY MANAGER WHO GOES OVERBOARD NEEDS TO FEEL THE PAIN—AND ON A PROMPT SCHEDULE.

If a manager overspends during one quarter, he or she can redeem the situation the next quarter by coming in at 10.9 or 10.8 percent, and thereby recover the lost bonus. On the other hand, if a manager consistently misses the mark for a year (maybe he or she has a long-suffering spouse!), we may put the *entire* annual raise into the bonus category. For the next year, none of it will come automatically. The person can get that money only by qualifying for the quarterly bonus.

But again: The key to hitting your wage target is *not* to pay cheap. It's rather to find and train the right people, and pay them adequately.

The second highest cost at the local level is rent. We go to great effort in choosing properties to make sure we're getting a good value. We don't want to work full-time for the benefit of the landlord.

We own very few properties ourselves. We've found that it makes better economic sense to lease buildings—usually an existing building, as I've mentioned before, that fits the Hobby Lobby format. If I have to look at the cost of buying a building, which would mean coming up with a 20 percent down payment, I say to myself, "For that much outlay of cash, I could open up a whole additional store somewhere and start making new money. Why should I tie up my funds in bricks and mortar?"

In choosing locations, it's easy to let your ego get carried away: *Here's the hot property in town; let's go for this as everyone else is doing.* This is a great way to spend unnecessarily. I'm not saying I want the cheapest building down a back alley somewhere, but a reasonable lease on a good location is often the wisest way to go.

Even then, we can never escape the requirements of local government, which sometimes make us scratch our heads. Building code inspectors, we've found, have an interesting way of changing their minds from day to day as we're rehabbing a building for store use. The fellow on Monday says one thing, but then a new guy comes around on Friday and requires something different. If we ask, "What about the previous directive?" he says, "Sorry. You'll have to do it my way."

In one 40,000-square-foot facility, we were informed that the building code required *fifteen* drinking fountains! My goodness, where would we even install that many? We pleaded for a variance, to no avail. So there they are today, all lined up on the wall. It's crazy.

Customers have looked at our list of store locations across the Upper Midwest and said, "Why don't you have any stores in Minneapolis or St. Paul? You're in other places in Minnesota; why not the capital area?" Well, the honest truth is that the Twin Cities tax rate is just too high for us. I'm not talking about sales tax, which comes out of the customers' pockets; I'm referring to the additional amount that businesses pay themselves. We would pay more per square foot in business taxes alone than we're paying for *rent* plus taxes and insurance in a number of other places. We can't afford to go there.

We could make the numbers work, I suppose, if we marked up all our prices to compensate for the extra tax load. But our merchandise is prepriced across the Hobby Lobby chain, and we have more than 100,000 items. To mark them all up just for Minneapolis–St. Paul, or any other expensive city, isn't feasible.

These are the kinds of things you have to watch at the store level. Any single thing has the power to tip over the boat.

When it comes to day-to-day operations, we hold store managers accountable for such things as housekeeping expenses. They have to go out and get bids from local cleaning companies, and since they don't always know what's a good price and what isn't, we help them. About five years ago we started giving them a per-square-foot guideline and said we were going to start watching that particular expense category. At the end of the year we published a list of all the stores, from low to high on a square-footage basis. Every store manager who hit or beat the guideline got a $500 bonus.

Amazingly (or maybe not so amazingly), in that first year, we saved more than half a million dollars on housekeeping costs. Today, the savings could be twice as much, since our chain has grown.

To me, the $500 in a store manager's pocket is money well spent, compared to the thousands and thousands he could otherwise waste by paying too much for floor care.

We've even started doing a similar monitoring of our window-washing expenses. The dollars here are smaller, but they still deserve attention. We've set a per-square-foot guideline on how much a store should pay to have its windows cleaned.

I doubt if very many retail companies in the world know exactly how many square feet of windows they have! Well, we know, because we've counted. That enables us to calculate the per-store cost of keeping them clean and, once again, form an annual ranking from low to high.

There's no bonus to earn in this case. The incentive for store managers is simply to not look bad on the report. And they take it seriously.

Why do I fuss about these kinds of expenses? Because deep down in my heart, I guess I haven't changed much from the young fellow who had to build his own store fixtures in the beginning because he couldn't afford to buy them. Barbara and I still laugh about the day we were driving home and spotted a large wooden spool, perhaps six feet in diameter, that the electric utility company had left along the roadside about a mile from our house. "Hey!—

this would make a good display counter for our store," we told each other.

> DEEP DOWN IN MY HEART, I GUESS I HAVEN'T CHANGED MUCH FROM THE YOUNG FELLOW WHO HAD TO BUILD HIS OWN STORE FIXTURES IN THE BEGINNING BECAUSE HE COULDN'T AFFORD TO BUY THEM.

I jumped out of the car, tipped the heavy spool up on edge, and began rolling it toward home. Barbara followed behind with the car's flasher lights going. We covered a few blocks at a slow speed. But then . . . the road began sloping downhill.

The spool started picking up speed. Soon it was getting away from me. I couldn't run fast enough to jump in front of it, and it would have been too heavy for me to stop anyway. Oh no!

The spool began trailing leftward toward the oncoming traffic. I panicked. I could just see some car getting smashed by this rumbling monster, and it would all be my fault.

Amazingly, the drivers swerved, and nobody got hit. Soon the spool bounced onto the opposite shoulder and flopped over onto its side with a thud. Both Barbara and I let out sighs of relief. "You better borrow a pickup truck to finish this job!" she admonished me through the open window of our car. And she was right.

But at least I had saved our store some money.

CHECKPOINT 3: WAREHOUSE AND CORPORATE EXPENSES

What's good for the goose is good for the gander. We can't expect the stores to control their costs if we don't do the same in Oklahoma City.

If you drove by our place out on Southwest Forty-fourth Street, you'd see a fairly utilitarian set of buildings. No executive towers of glass and chrome; in fact, we're all on the ground level. No neon signs glowing in the night. No executive parking garage; my car sits out there baking in the Oklahoma sun like everybody else's. In fact, the only reserved spaces near the door are for visitors.

> NO EXECUTIVE PARKING GARAGE; MY CAR SITS OUT THERE BAKING IN THE OKLAHOMA SUN LIKE EVERYBODY ELSE'S. IN FACT, THE ONLY RESERVED SPACES NEAR THE DOOR ARE FOR VISITORS.

The biggest slice of our corporate payroll is in our warehouse—a vast complex of 3 million square feet, with more than 350 truck loading bays, that employs 1,200 people. Every week I get a report that shows exactly how much product (at cost) was shipped out for the total number of hours worked by the warehouse crew. It's a measure of productivity.

In 1999, we were shipping $283 worth of product for every hour worked. The next year, we improved to $353, then $385, then $499, and then $538. Part of that improvement was due to a sophisticated conveyor system we installed in the warehouse. We also invested in more motorized carts so people wouldn't have to do so much walking from bin to bin. Yes, the conveyor system cost us $25 million, but that was a onetime purchase that will help us a long time.

By the way, nobody lost their job due to the mechanical improvements. Everyone just got more efficient at what they do, as shown by the annual numbers, and the overall growth of the chain kept them busy. They are now able to load twenty trailers at a time. This also allowed us to raise our wage scales for warehouse work.

All of this came about because we started measuring our output, thinking about it, and taking steps to make it better.

Once the trucks are loaded, we need to get them to their destinations at the lowest possible price. This is what led us to create our own trucking company. We are currently running about a hundred tractors, with a fleet of three hundred trailers (roughly one per store). We have our own maintenance facility beside our warehouse. We buy our own fuel in bulk, and we put oversize fuel tanks on our tractors so our drivers don't have to stop on the road and buy so much of somebody else's more expensive diesel.

We buy our own oil in bulk, and tires as well. We do our own truck washing. To set up for all this, we visited perhaps a dozen different truck operations around the country, asking them what's smart and what's not. This led us to design the maintenance building accordingly, with extra-wide doors so the mirrors don't get knocked around, with drainages underneath for oil changes, and so forth.

Yes, it was a lot of work. But anybody else who would haul freight for us was obviously going to make a profit, so why not keep that money ourselves?

In fact, we're pretty active in the hauling business for other companies now on our return trips to Oklahoma City. The term is "back-hauling": We load up somebody else's goods and deliver them for a fee instead of driving home empty. This has become a multimillion-dollar operation for us.

A much different kind of headquarters expense happens in the front office: advertising decisions. In the early days John Seward, my partner, hand-lettered this flyer himself for door-to-door distribution. Talk about low-budget advertising!

Once again, we want the best results at the least possible expense. That's why we don't do glossy, full-color inserts that fall out of the Sunday paper. People ask me about that all the time: "Why don't you do those tabloids on Sunday like everybody else does?"

I reply, "To talk is expensive. Every time you say something to the public, you need to get your money back in results. I've just found a cheaper way to get the same results." That cheaper way is the black-and-white ads we run every Sunday within the regular pages of the newspaper itself. We concentrate on coming up with fifty-two good ads each year that run one-third to one-half page in size. Then, starting in early November and on

An Early Hobby Lobby Ad

through Christmas, we kick it up to a full page each week.

Because most of our competitors are publicly owned companies that are required to publish financial statements for their stockholders, I can see what they spend on advertising. We, by contrast, are spending about half their rate. We feel if we consistently give the customer good value, we don't have to shout so loud from week to week.

I kind of chuckle every time I get a promotion in the mail from the main printing company that does glossy tabloids. Over the years they've sent me samples of their work for eight different competitors of mine, seeking to get my account as well. The only trouble is, five out of those eight are no longer in business, and a sixth is currently in bankruptcy proceedings! Shouldn't that tell them something?

Advertising can't do everything, of course. If you advertise something unfamiliar to the customer, you're wasting your money. If you say, "Ceramic vases—$2.99," well, the customer can't tell whether that's a bargain or not. She can't tell whether it would fit her home's particular style or not. She has to see it first.

That's why we advertise whole categories instead of individual items. Better to say, "All ceramics 30% off this week." That piques the interest of the consumer to come take a look.

There are a few exceptions to this rule. If at Christmastime we say, "100-bulb light strings—$1.77," the customer can immediately picture what we're talking about. But the vast majority of our store's inventory is harder to describe in four words or less. Therefore, it's better for us to convey the general idea of *super selection, super savings* on large, generic categories to get people up and out of their chairs. Our strategy is more inclusive.

A hidden expense that can really kill a retail company is interest. I regret having to take hard-earned dollars from the sales floor and hand them over to a bank. I look forward to the day when Hobby Lobby will have zero debt. We're not that far away even now. I'd much rather put earnings toward expanding the business and funding charitable programs that could really use it for good.

Cost control in an organization should not be viewed as a chore. It is rather an indication of priority. What's important enough to get us to spend our limited amount of resources, and what isn't? No company in the world has "money to burn," as the phrase goes. The most high-flying corporation today can hit the skids within a year or two if it doesn't watch the outflow. Far better to manage the expenses with eyes wide open, keeping the proportions in line day after day, month after month, year after year.

CHAPTER 6

WHAT COMPUTERS DON'T KNOW

Before going any further, I'd better stop and explain why Hobby Lobby doesn't have scanner technology at our checkouts. Many people wonder about this. They think we're stuck in the previous century, or else we're just plain dumb. One person wrote me to say, "What are you—Amish?"

No, I'm not Amish, although I can think of several reasons to respect that group of people. Their communities actually do pretty well in business despite the lack of high-tech gizmos. And when an oil crisis hits, sending gasoline prices through the roof and causing the rest of us to panic, the Amish horse-drawn buggies just keep rolling right on down the road.

One of my favorite quotes about technology comes from esteemed business guru Peter Drucker: "The computer is a moron." Another expert whose name I have forgotten put it only a little more kindly when he said, "The computer is like having an extremely precocious eight-year-old hanging around your office. He's very smart about the few things he knows in life, and he's forever asking questions—but sometimes you just want to tell him to shut up!"

I will put it even more nicely than those two: A computer is a great rearview mirror. It can tell you all kinds of things about where you've been last week, last month, and last year—how much you sold of what. But I am a *merchant*, and merchants have to look *forward*. They have to go where the computer has not yet been.

A COMPUTER IS A GREAT REARVIEW MIRROR . . . BUT I AM A MERCHANT, AND MERCHANTS HAVE TO LOOK FORWARD. THEY HAVE TO GO WHERE THE COMPUTER HAS NOT YET BEEN.

WHAT A MERCHANT NEEDS— AND DOESN'T NEED

Don't get me wrong: Hobby Lobby uses computers in many ways. I have a computer-generated financial profit-and-loss statement on every one of our 300-plus stores. We know exactly how many of each of our 46,000 standing items left our warehouse last month, and the month before that, and the six-month trend, and the previous six-month trend. Our stores transmit their refill orders by computer to the warehouse, and the computer organizes the pick list for the crew getting ready to load trucks. Every box has a bar code to help guide it toward the right outgoing truck.

We have great people in our IS (information systems) department. But my son Steve, who oversees this group, has made clear to them that we do not intend to be on the cutting edge—because that's where the blood is. Their job is not to be far-out. Their job is to stick to the basics.

I don't need to know how many employees across the chain wore blue shirts last Tuesday. I don't need to know whether we have more Smiths or Johnsons on our payroll. All I want to know are the core indicators of the business, in simple one-page reports that I can understand. If this is boring work for an IS person, then he or she probably ought to go get a job at a think tank somewhere instead.

I'm looking for solid, practical technology that has been proved for years in somebody else's business. I'm not looking for things like the little button on my car that opens and closes the trunk. I'm sure the engineer who invented it is really proud, but what was the point? My hand works just fine to get the trunk lid up and down! If the little button malfunctions, it's going to cost me a bunch of money to get it fixed.

> **I'M NOT LOOKING FOR THINGS LIKE THE LITTLE BUTTON ON MY CAR THAT OPENS AND CLOSES THE TRUNK. I'M SURE THE ENGINEER WHO INVENTED IT IS REALLY PROUD, BUT WHAT WAS THE POINT?**

I want to keep things as basic as possible. I started out in business long ago giving my sales numbers in a shoebox to my accountant. Today we may use a more electronic transmittal method, but I want the results to be as clear now as they were then.

WHY WE DON'T USE BAR CODES

I've taken so much grief for not having a POS (point-of-sale) system that scans and records information from bar codes on the product, that I finally made a list of the reasons why. Here are just a few of them:

1. *Human beings can't read a bar code.* Those thin black lines mean nothing to a customer who's trying to figure out the price of something. Only the scanner knows (assuming it has been properly programmed). So the store has to post the price in plain English some other way: a label on the shelf, for example. If one customer picks up an item and then puts it down again in the wrong bin, the next customer can be misled as to the real price—which leads to a dispute at the cash register. "Your sign said this was 79 cents." "No, I'm sorry, but the computer says it's 99 cents." "Well, that's not what I saw!" And things deteriorate from there.

Some retailers put scanners in their aisles so a customer can walk over and hold up the bar code at just the right angle to find what the item costs. Everything I've read says that customers don't like doing this; it's a foreign practice to them.

2. *A lot of our product comes from cottage industries in Asia that couldn't mark their goods with bar codes if they tried.* Can you imagine our buyer saying to the Philippine maker of papier-mâché boxes, "I'll take sixty dozen of those—but you'll have to bar-code them"? That would kill the deal right there, or we'd have to use the services of a trading company, which would add another 15–25 percent to the cost of goods.

3. *Inventory control by computer is not as accurate as you think.* Yes, the computer can keep track of what gets scanned at the cash register. But what about items that are

shoplifted? What about items that are dropped and broken? The computer has no easy way of knowing about these disappearances. It blithely goes on telling the staff they have such-and-such, when in fact they don't. In stores like ours that carry a myriad of items in quantities of just one or two or three, we could easily have none on the shelf and not know it.

I have a vendor right now who sells us needles. He says he can ship only 40 percent of what I ordered, even though he claims he has everything in his warehouse, but "the computer messed me up." He is just sitting there hoping I'll be patient and wait for him to get his act together instead of going off to one of his competitors.

In our stores, we know how much inventory we have because we keep track the old-fashioned way: *We count.* We actually eyeball the goods—every week. Our people stand there in the aisle with a printout showing every item's "basic stock level" (a two-month supply). They know if they see less than half the "basic stock" number, they're supposed to reorder now. That way, there will be plenty of overlap—unless something strange occurs, like a customer coming in and buying out the whole lot.

> IN OUR STORES, WE KNOW HOW MUCH INVENTORY WE HAVE BECAUSE WE KEEP TRACK THE OLD-FASHIONED WAY: WE COUNT. WE ACTUALLY EYEBALL THE GOODS—EVERY WEEK.

Some people say, "Oh my goodness, you must be wasting a huge amount of money on extra wages to have all those

employees counting all those stickers and brushes and ornaments every week!" Well, as I told you in the previous chapter, we spend an average of only 11 percent of our revenue on
store wages, which is well in line with our industry. Plus,
we're not spending millions on POS hardware, software, and
a panel of expensive programmers to maintain it. As a result,
Hobby Lobby is consistently profitable, year after year—and
more profitable than our competitors. I'm happy with how it
all works out.

4. *Employees take more pride in their work when they
know they are in charge, not some faceless machine.* The
woman in charge of the floral department in Kearney,
Nebraska, knows that she controls her own destiny. Having
the goods on display is entirely up to her. If a customer wants
a bolt of blue ribbon and there is none to be had, she knows
it's her fault. She can't pass the blame on to some computer
somewhere that "forgot" to order a replenishment.

As a result, our people invest a tremendous amount of
tender loving care in the departments they manage. They
want their operation to look good and be ready for business
at all times. That's why the average Hobby Lobby consistently runs 95 percent in stock on all our thousands of items.

5. *Customer service is better.* Because of this direct
attention to the stock, our people are better prepared to
answer customer questions. They know right away if we
have an item or not, where it is, which colors are available,
and what it costs. They don't have to go consult a computer
somewhere.

6. *The time savings at checkout is minimal—and easily
squandered.* The difference between a checker scanning an
item electronically or keying in the price manually is frac-
tions of a second. If a customer is buying six items, what

have we saved—four seconds? Throw in just one glitch—
one missing price in the computer, one bar code that can't be
read because it's smudged—and *poof!* goes the time savings.

We tell our store managers that if checkout lines get
long, don't blame it on the lack of a POS system; just open
up another lane and deploy another checker. Do the simple,
immediate thing to fix the problem.

My wife and I shop at any number of other stores that *do*
have POS systems, and their checkout lines can get frustrat-
ingly long too. The bottleneck is not so much the technology
as it is simply having too few open lanes for customers to use.
We all need to do a better job on that score.

7. *Reprogramming the computer for sales would take
a huge effort in our case, because we put so many individual items on sale every week.* We don't just advertise a few
items on sale, like a grocery store or mass merchandiser. We
discount whole categories—all the jewelry-making department, for example, or all the garden items. These can run
into thousands of individual SKUs (stock-keeping units).
Next week it will be a different department. In our case it's
far simpler for the checkout people to do these discounts
because they know the departments well.

I've seen more than one investigative feature on TV
shows such as *20/20* where a reporter goes into a store, buys
something, and finds that the computer has not been cor-
rectly programmed. The advertised price was one thing, and
what the computer actually said was something higher.

8. *Twenty million dollars is a lot of money.* That's
approximately what it would cost to buy and implement a
POS system for the Hobby Lobby chain. And would we be
any better off, any more profitable than we are right now? I
doubt it.

I don't insist that this view is right for every business. In fact, we have a spin-off operation called Mardel, an educational/office supply/Christian bookstore chain of nearly twenty stores that does use POS. Their sources are much more standardized than Hobby Lobby's, for one thing. Very little comes from overseas.

But even there, we refuse to let machines run the business. We insist that computers remain our servants, not our masters. And that's my point: We are in the business of offering tangible home and craft items to real, live human beings. That's why we come to work in the morning. We are *not* in the business of seeing what fancy cartwheels the computer can spin today. We really don't care about that.

> WE ARE IN THE BUSINESS OF OFFERING TANGIBLE HOME AND CRAFT ITEMS TO REAL, LIVE HUMAN BEINGS . . . WE ARE NOT IN THE BUSINESS OF SEEING WHAT FANCY CARTWHEELS THE COMPUTER CAN SPIN TODAY. WE REALLY DON'T CARE ABOUT THAT.

If computers can help us do our primary work better, we welcome them. If they can't, would they please step aside?

People say, "Oh, computers don't make mistakes. It's the people who run them." Or, "It's the software that messed up." Whatever the combination of hardware, software, and humanity, it has to enable the making of good decisions in the real world. All else is a waste of time and money.

Kirk Humphreys, former mayor of Oklahoma City, was telling me about the wholesale business he had before he got into politics. The total IS department was three people. For decades his family earned a good living from the operation.

They eventually sold to another owner who brought in a lot of technology and expanded the IS group to thirty people. The business has since closed its doors.

I hear these stories nearly every month, it seems. They remind me to keep my head in the game, not expecting computers to do my job.

In retail, there's nothing wrong with getting your hands dirty. I like what Al Ries and Jack Trout wrote in their book, *The 22 Immutable Laws of Marketing*:

> Marketing managers have to know what's happening in the marketplace. They have to be down at the front of the mud in the battle. They have to know what's working and what isn't. They have to be involved.
>
> Because of the high cost of mistakes, management can't afford to delegate important marketing decisions . . .
>
> It's hard to find that single move [of genius] if you're hanging around headquarters and not involved in the process.[1]

I read once about a major New York book publisher that had an unusual policy for its editorial department: Every second week of December, at the peak of the Christmas rush, all the editors shut down their computers and got kicked out of their cushy, high-rise offices to go work in a Manhattan bookstore. For a full six days they were on their feet behind the counter, answering questions, watching customers paw through books as they decided to buy this one and ignore that one. The editors went home every night exhausted, of course, not only from the standing but also from the noise, the flurry of constant activity, and the juggling of tasks all day long. It was good for them to see where their beloved manuscripts finally ended up.

To be in the thick of the action, looking at merchandise, touching it, feeling it, smelling it, turning it upside down, and sensing what the customer thinks of it . . . this is retail.

Chapter 7

Keep It Simple

About two miles from our corporate office, at the corner of West Reno and MacArthur and next door to a Super Wal-Mart, sits Hobby Lobby Store Number 2. It is 55,000 square feet in size, has a workforce of 40, and does about $5 million a year in sales. In other words, it's pretty much a typical Hobby Lobby—no better, no worse than others in the chain.

I stop by to visit that store just about every day I'm in town. Not because there's anything wrong. The manager and the staff do a fine job. They just give me a wave and keep going about their normal business, because the CEO's appearance is old hat by now.

The same is true for our three-dozen merchandise buyers. They're always in Store Number 2, nosing around whatever department is their specific responsibility.

Why do we come so often?

Because what happens in this store is astoundingly similar to what happens in every other Hobby Lobby across the nation. It's a microcosm of the whole. The way Oklahoma

City customers respond is not all that different from customers north, south, east, and west, from Fargo to Houston and from Charlotte to Grand Junction, Colorado. What they buy and don't buy is surprisingly consistent.

I talked to one executive at a competitor with an elaborate POS system. After poring over data for hours and days on end, doing cross-tabulations, checking for all kinds of variables, he told me, "You know what, David? It's all the same." In our particular field, customers are customers pretty much wherever you go in America.

We could spend a ton of money flying around the country doing individualized research in various stores. It would be interesting, and we'd see a lot of scenery. But the numbers would not be all that much more enlightening than what we already get by driving over to 6104 West Reno.

ONE LIST FITS (NEARLY) ALL

This has led us to keep things simple by stocking every store with basically the same inventory. There is almost no variation from one town to another. The only difference is in *how much* of each item goes into a given store.

Three numbers tell the whole tale:

— What is the total sales volume of this store? Does it sell $3 million in a year's time? $4 million? $5 million?

— What slice of the entire Hobby Lobby chain does this represent?

— How many of a particular item do we sell across the whole chain in a month?

With those three numbers, I can tell how much of each item to put into each store. This becomes the "basic stock level" I mentioned in the last chapter. No need for guessing and debating and crystal ball gazing. If we sell 3,000 of the 9 x 12 ebony picture frames across the chain in a month, and a certain store does 0.4 percent of the company's total sales volume in a year, then that means they should sell 12 ebony picture frames each month. The "basic stock level" therefore becomes 24, and when the frame department worker notices during the weekly check that he's down to 12, it's time to reorder.

Is that simple enough?

The same is true for shipping in our "send-out" merchandise, the seasonal and onetime items that we push into the stores. We look at a store's percentage of overall sales volume, multiply by what we think we can sell across the chain, and that's what the store receives, no questions asked. There's no need for an elaborate ladder of "A" stores, "B" stores, and "C" stores like some companies have; the sales ratio tells the tale for everyone.

There is no picking and choosing at the local level. No store manager is allowed to say, "Well, I don't personally like that item, so I'd rather not carry it." Or, "Well, we don't have room for that." Yes, you do. A Hobby Lobby is a Hobby Lobby anywhere, and there are more important things to do with our time than fiddle with the product mix.

When I used to be a store manager for TG&Y in my early days, I could easily spend forty hours a week on paperwork. I would beat my brains out deciding how much to order of this, how much of that, how much we were carrying over from last time, on and on. I had to work at least sixty hours a week because of all the other duties calling for my attention.

At Hobby Lobby, if we tried to make localized decisions on all 46,000 year-round items times 320 stores, that would be a staggering 14,720,000 stock decisions! Instead, our simple system takes care of all that—with an impressive fill rate. It's all "ratio-to-sales," as we call it. As a result, the average Hobby Lobby store manager spends no more than thirty minutes a day on paperwork. The rest of the time, he or she is free to be out on the sales floor, talking to customers and coaching the team.

> THE AVERAGE HOBBY LOBBY STORE MANAGER SPENDS NO MORE THAN THIRTY MINUTES A DAY ON PAPERWORK.

A FEW EXCEPTIONS

Are there any exceptions to this simple uniformity of product allocation across the chain? Yes, to name just a few examples:

— Something with a bluebonnet on it sells better in Texas, obviously.

— Something with a chili sells better in New Mexico.

— Something with a sunflower sells better in Kansas.

— Outdoor Christmas decorations sell better in the warm-weather South than the frigid North. Somehow the guys in Wisconsin aren't as inspired to go climbing up on the roof in December with a string of lights as the guys in Mississippi.

So we make manual adjustments in how we stock these stores on those items and a few others. But we are determined that the exception shouldn't become the rule. For 99 percent of our items, "ratio-to-sales" works just fine and shouldn't be complicated.

I don't know if that's how they teach you to do it at Harvard Business School—I never got to go there. In fact, I never even made it to college. I just learned in the trenches of day-to-day retail by hunting for the straightest, simplest way to get the job done.

ONE SUPPLY CHAIN

As you've already realized, virtually all merchandise arrives on a truck from Oklahoma City once a week. If a store transmits its weekly order on Monday, the truck will roll in sometime Tuesday with the goods. Everything is there at one time, listed on one document.

We've hired store managers from other retail operations that tell horror stories about receiving as many as seventy or more different UPS shipments from various vendors in a given day. That's seventy invoices and seventy possibilities for shortage, not to mention all kinds of excess cardboard to deal with. That company thinks it is being efficient by drop-shipping straight from the supplier instead of going through a central warehouse, but it doesn't see the complexities at the receiving end for an already harried manager.

Another problem is that most suppliers have a minimum order of, say, $100. So what if a store is out of white thread? Is it going to order $100 worth? Its employees are more likely to wait until they're out of three or four different colors, and then make up an order that will satisfy the minimum. In the meantime, sales are being lost every day.

The Hobby Lobby system lets the store order as few as a dozen spools of thread from our warehouse—no problem. That's why I believe it is more efficient to haul a load of thread from a mill in North Carolina to Oklahoma City, then disperse it out to individual stores as needed, even though it may sound otherwise. We stay in control this way. We don't have store managers buying things they don't really need or want because of some artificial constraint.

And, in fact, we get the thread cheaper because we buy in bulk. The mill would much rather sell us a big lot than have to sprinkle out three hundred parcels to each of our stores. We make sure its price reflects that.

As a matter of fact, the freight from North Carolina may not cost us much extra, because one of our own trucks may be back-hauling on that route after delivering products to Hobby Lobby stores in that state.

There are only three exceptions to this rule of central shipping:

1. Sewing patterns
2. Greeting cards
3. Posters

Each of these unique product lines has a continuous-flow replenishment system, whereby the supplier is set up to stock thousands and thousands of outlets on an ongoing basis. If you sell an anniversary card, they'll replace it with a different anniversary card next time. Similarly, the patterns and the posters are constantly changing, almost like a magazine rack that has new titles every month.

We allow these suppliers to service our stores directly. Occasionally, the greeting card companies give us headaches by putting in cards that are risqué or off-color, in violation of the standards we've set. We have to remind them of what's acceptable at Hobby Lobby.

Everything else comes through the central supply chain.

OTHER WAYS TO SIMPLIFY

At the home office, we believe in keeping things simple just as much as in the stores.

We ship everything out of one warehouse complex here on Southwest Forty-fourth Street, for example. Could we have multiple warehouses in various parts of the country? Yes, I suppose—but so far I'm not convinced it would actually save us money. Carrying as many items as we do (close to 100,000) would require a tremendous dispersal of inventory to the various locations in the beginning. When a forty-foot shipping container of photo frames arrives from Asia, we'd have to break it apart and start trucking it off in all directions without actually getting it to its ultimate destination anyway, which is the individual store. Then we'd have the problem of running out of something in one warehouse while another had a surplus. The back-and-forth of it all could become a nightmare.

At this point, I'd rather pay the price of our trucks hauling goods a few extra miles from week to week in order to keep the warehouse function centralized and controllable. The downside risk of spreading out seems greater to me than the current method.

When it comes to policies and procedures, I'm always pushing to keep things simple. Somebody asked me once what was the secret of our success, and I replied only half-jokingly, "We refuse to hire more than one attorney per each billion dollars in annual sales!" Actually, I stretched the truth a bit there; we have two attorneys on staff, and we're not quite up to $2 billion yet. So no more lawyers for a while.

Our attorneys, like most, are conservative, as they should be, which is why I tease them all the time. I'll say, "You know, if we didn't open this new store, we'd be sure nobody would slip and fall on the sidewalk!" and then we'll laugh together. I want them to do a prudent job of protecting us, but we're not going to go hide in a cave somewhere, either. Business is all about taking risks. They just have to be calculated risks.

The larger we get, the more time I seem to spend fighting bureaucracy. I just can't see the sense of bogging down the busy store manager with a ton of paperwork. As you can imagine, the attorneys and I haggle about this from time to time. "Is this prevention or stipulation *really* necessary?" I ask. "What's the worst thing that could happen if we didn't put out this new memo?"

Recently a letter was prepared telling all store managers to ship back a certain seasonal product because it infringed on somebody's patent. I said, "No, don't do that. Just tell 'em to throw it away. Don't bother the store manager any more than is absolutely necessary." The stores don't exist for us; we exist for them. We're here to do everything we can to make their lives simpler and easier so they can focus on the real work.

Too many companies discourage their store managers by piling on all kinds of extraneous requirements. The person opens his e-mail or regular mail in the morning and sighs,

"These headquarters types have no clue what my life is like." I am determined that we are not going to do that. We're going to be realistic, not idealistic.

The more difficult you make a system, the less likelihood it's going to happen. We are not looking for the perfect method for every task; we're looking for the realistic method. And usually, that's the simplest one.

> WE ARE NOT LOOKING FOR THE
> PERFECT METHOD FOR EVERY TASK;
> WE'RE LOOKING FOR THE REALISTIC
> METHOD. AND USUALLY, THAT'S THE
> SIMPLEST ONE.

ONE VOICE, PLEASE

Kenny Haywood, our executive vice president, and I are both old store managers at heart; in fact, I hired him as a stock boy when he was just sixteen years old. Kenny and I came up through the ranks together. We know what it feels like on the other end.

Maybe that's why the two of us continually hammer about what goes out to our store managers today. We read every piece of mail before it leaves the home office. If a communication is too long and complicated, we send it back for rewriting. "You can say this shorter," we'll tell a buyer or other person in the home office.

The truth of the matter is, I rarely read a letter on my desk that's longer than one page. If somebody sends me a six-page letter, I automatically hand it to Ruby Race, my longtime assistant, for screening and summarizing.

Sometimes she'll come back with a slight smile on her face and say, "Basically, they hate your guts." Well, okay—that I understand. I'll then ask one follow-up question: "Did we do anything wrong?" If so, I truly want to know. But, please, spare me the long oration.

A few years back, I began to realize that our growth was pushing beyond what Kenny could directly oversee. All the district managers (each responsible for some twenty stores) were answering directly to him, and I could see we needed to divide the company into three divisions—north, south, and east—with a regional vice president for each.

But that scared me, because I'd come from a company that had multiple divisions going their separate ways. They had even created separate buying departments, which was absurd.

I made it clear that the three regional vice presidents would not make rules. In fact, they would not even communicate with their stores unless it was to reiterate company policy. I told them, "If somebody has a good idea, that's wonderful—share it *upward* so we can pass it along to the entire chain. Don't just send out your idea to your one-third of the company; we can all benefit from this. Move it up, and we'll move it out."

In this way, we maintain one voice to the entire organization. We won't allow a babble of conflicting voices to rumble around the chain. We are one entity.

DARE TO BE DIFFERENT

As I said in the opening chapter, systems are not number one. They are number four—after serving God, serving people, and being a merchant. Systems exist only to make the first three possible.

> ## SYSTEMS ARE NOT NUMBER ONE. THEY ARE NUMBER FOUR—AFTER SERVING GOD, SERVING PEOPLE, AND BEING A MERCHANT. SYSTEMS EXIST ONLY TO MAKE THE FIRST THREE POSSIBLE.

Many systems, if not watched carefully, will end up tying the hands of a merchant. I am ever on guard against this. I don't hesitate to break the long-standing tradition of how other businesses have always done things.

I love the example of Southwest Airlines saying, "We're not going to give our passengers a seat assignment." *What?! You can't do that—every other airline gives a seat assignment.* Well, Southwest says, "Not us."

Why not? Because their studies showed that the process of giving each customer an assigned seat, changing it around for those who are unhappy, and getting everybody into the proper seat takes an extra ten minutes for every boarding. Their planes would be sitting on the ground an extra ten minutes as a result. What's ten minutes? Well, management calculated that to operate the Southwest network with this additional ground time would require buying *thirty additional aircraft—at $36 million apiece!*

They said no way. You can complain if you want, and you can take your business to another airline if you want. But they're not complicating their system. And the truth is, Southwest remains one of the most profitable airlines in the sky.

Besides, have you noticed how mature, intelligent, even college-educated passengers still can't seem to park themselves in seat 11D as assigned? They plop down in the general neighborhood, and then the next passenger comes along and has to push them out, and the whole thing becomes a circus. So what was the value of seat assignments in the first place?

Whether in airlines or the craft business . . . just keep it simple.

CHAPTER 8

WHAT COMMITTEES DON'T KNOW

———— ⌇ ————

The game we love here in North America called football is not widely known in the rest of the world. When I'm in an overseas hotel and turn on the TV to watch sports, I see something called *futbol*, but it's what you and I know as soccer. Of course, internationals argue that in our game, hardly anyone touches the *ball* with their *foot* (which is true). They think we ought to call ours "tackleball" or even "throwball" instead.

I love the story of the Englishman who was visiting here and was taken to an American football game. After sitting in the stadium for three hours, watching all the huddles and scrimmages and referees handing out penalties, he was asked afterward for his comment. He said, "Well, this incorporates two of the worst elements of American culture, namely, violence . . . and committee meetings."

Yes, indeed. We Americans seem to love our committees. In some of our state legislatures, they even have, in addition to committees on transportation and agriculture and education, a committee on committees. Apparently, their job is to organize all the other committees.

The business world is committee-crazy too. We sometimes give them alternate names, like "task force" or "cross-functional team," claiming they're more effective than old-fashioned committees. Maybe so, maybe not.

At Hobby Lobby, we're not wild about committees or the lengthy meetings they seem to require. In fact, back when I was a store manager, I never held a staff meeting at all. That's because I've always hated to get up in front of a crowd. I'd much rather go around to twelve people and give them the same message than have to stand up and address them as a group.

> **AT HOBBY LOBBY, WE'RE NOT WILD ABOUT COMMITTEES OR THE LENGTHY MEETINGS THEY SEEM TO REQUIRE.**

On the first Wednesday of each month at our headquarters, we do have five meetings, one right after another—and that's it. No more until the next month. The meetings are:

1. Officers and buyers, about sixty people in all. We spend about forty-five minutes or less going over general news, reporting on an overseas buying trip, maybe even sharing something funny.

2. The officers leave, and the thirty-six buyers stay so we can firm up what's going into our weekly ads three months down the road.

3. Next come the eight merchandising managers, or just the buyers for Hemispheres, our new furnishings start-up.

4. At noon is a lunch for the officers and leaders of our sister companies, such as Worldwood; Crafts, Etc.!; Greco Frame & Supply; Mardel Christian & Educational Supply; etc.

5. Finally, just the directors meet to set policy for all the companies. The directors are all family members, and we'll talk about what employee benefits to declare, for example, or what corporate donations to make.

By mid-afternoon, we're done for the month. People do far more of their work by talking to each other informally, solving the problem at hand. Two or three of us will gather for an eight-minute conversation and then move on. Generally speaking, I don't want more than three people making any final decision. If it's a real estate decision, it's the real estate director, my son Steve (president), and myself. If it's operations, it's Steve, Kenny Haywood, and maybe the attorney if there's some legal angle to it.

This is all part of our corporate culture of flexibility, staying fluid, moving to adapt to the ever-changing environment of retail.

At the monthly officers' lunch, I don't want twelve people sitting around the table fussing about what the stores should do, when four of them have never even been store managers. That would be a terrible use of time. Instead, we focus on our overall direction.

In my opinion, a company gets stiff and arthritic when it focuses too much on its structure. Every hour that people spend fighting for the place and authority of their office or their particular department is an hour lost to the real work, which is buying and selling. When committees and other bodies drift into a life of their own, independent of one another, the momentum fades. The bureaucracy grows, and the dysfunction multiplies.

The German automaker Porsche once took out a dramatic, two-page ad in national American magazines to feature this quotation from their leader, Ferdinand Porsche:

> Committees are, by nature, timid. They are based on the premise of safety in numbers; content to survive inconspicuously, rather than take risks and move independently ahead. Without independence, with the freedom for new ideas to be tried, to fail, and to ultimately succeed, the world will not move ahead, but live in fear of its own potential.

I don't have many talents personally, but I do think one talent God gave me was to see the bigger picture, to grasp how it all comes together. People kid me about my tendency to repeat the phrase "the big picture" all the time—well, it's important. This organization is like a human body. If you have one arm flailing around independently of the rest and a knee jerking out to the side every few seconds, you have a serious and tragic disorder. The body parts need to work in harmony with each other on a second-by-second basis. It's a rhythm thing, and formal meetings to talk about rhythm are often counterproductive. Better to make it happen on the fly.

I don't want Hobby Lobby to be like American football, stopping every twenty seconds for another "committee meeting." I want us to look like Manchester United or one of the other great soccer teams—ever fluid, ever in motion, ever moving toward the goal.

FREEDOM TO GET THE BEST VALUE

Let me give an example: our thirty-six merchandise buyers. These are the people who make the all-important selections of what's going to appear in the stores.

They have no restraints of any kind. They may travel to any country of the world looking for value. They don't have to pass anything by a committee. If they think this blue ceramic clock or that five-shelf mahogany unit for the den is a good choice at a workable price—that's it. They buy it on the spot and send it heading for the stores.

> OUR THIRTY-SIX MERCHANDISE BUYERS HAVE NO RESTRAINTS OF ANY KIND. THEY MAY TRAVEL TO ANY COUNTRY OF THE WORLD LOOKING FOR VALUE. THEY DON'T HAVE TO PASS ANYTHING BY A COMMITTEE.

They don't even have a firm budget to live within. Yes, we give them guidelines—but if they see a hot deal, they know they are free to ignore the budget. Grab it, and let's go!

They don't have to gum up the works by waiting on a bar code, as I explained previously. And their choices don't have to fit into some preordained plan-o-gram like many other retailers use. A plan-o-gram is a rigid drawing of what a display should look like, with a designated shelf or pegboard hook for every individual item. You hand it to the store personnel and say, "Here—make your department look exactly like this." These plan-o-grams take a lot of work, which is why they get updated only about every six months.

We don't do that. Yes, we take pictures of attractive merchandising and send them to the stores as suggestions. But we leave display decisions up to the local people, thereby preserving flexibility.

And at any time of the year, if a buyer comes up with a hot new product to offer the customers, we can accommodate it. We're not locked into a plan-o-gram.

As one manufacturer told a trade reporter about Hobby Lobby, "They can react quickly. If something looks good, they'll find room for it and buy it now—not for a year from now. [They don't require] 'tests'—they're buyers, and good buyers sometimes have to . . . stick their necks out."

Another vendor put the same idea in different words by saying, "Hobby Lobby has consistently shown fast decision-making capability on new lines. As a result, it is often the first to market with these new programs."

A third vendor wrote:

I have been trying to get new product into a couple of chains this season, and the strain and sweat and complication and difficulty and aggravation of it all makes me realize how nice it is to work directly with Hobby Lobby.

The way you add product and then merchandise it makes so much sense to us. Working with you has always been easy and straightforward.

You buy the product from us at a fair price and then assume the risk of selling it and making a profit. That's exactly what we do. We manufacture our product at a fair cost and take the risk of selling it for a profit.

Some of these chains complicate matters so much,

and toss around so many percentages, that it's impossible
to TRACK if you're making a profit, let alone actually
MAKE one.

What he's talking about is the common practice of other
companies to get a price on a product and then start asking
for discounts. "Well, in order to advertise your product, I
need another 5 percent off," and on and on ad nauseum. All
of this requires extra paperwork.

Vendors have told us, "Some company buyers will actually ask me to *raise* my prices at the beginning, so then we
can go through this dance and they can show their bosses
what wonderful discounts they negotiated!"

We don't do any of this monkeying around. We simply
say, "Give us your best price, and that's it. Let's keep it
simple."

Of course, our buyers know that there is only so much
space in a store, so they can't buy everything in sight. A
slower-moving item may have to be dropped to make room
for the newly discovered attraction. That's okay—I'm glad
for buyers to make those trade-offs.

WHAT ABOUT MISTAKES?

If all this sounds like a high-wire act that is prone to devas-
tating falls, I would quickly admit that we've made our
share of bad decisions over the years.

I fully trust the taste and judgment of these thirty-six
buyers. And yes, sometimes I walk through the aisles of
Store Number 2 and say, "Why in the world did So-and-
so buy *that*?" But I don't go chew out the person. I give
the product time to see how the customers respond. And

sometimes I am totally wrong, and the customers love it! I fully expect buyers to make mistakes from time to time. If they don't, they're being too cautious. I've made buying mistakes myself. One time I got excited about papier-mâché chickens out of the Philippines. I was like Herbert Hoover running for president back in 1928; I could envision a chicken in every kitchen in America. So I bought several containerloads.

> ### I FULLY EXPECT BUYERS TO MAKE MISTAKES FROM TIME TO TIME. IF THEY DON'T, THEY'RE BEING TOO CAUTIOUS.

Well, they did terribly in the marketplace. The old-timers still remind me about those chickens once in a while! We all laugh about it now.

None of us can pick winners 100 percent of the time. The goal instead is to maintain a designated margin on an entire *category* of product. The average buyer is overseeing some 3,000 SKUs ("stock-keeping units") and spending around $20 million a year. They know that if the whole cluster of SKUs delivers its margin target in the end, everything is fine.

This frees them to take risks. They know their mandate: "Get the very best value you can for the customer." If this means bringing in something we've never carried before, that's fine as long as it belongs in a Hobby Lobby environment. If this means taking an expensive trip to Thailand or Slovakia, so be it. We don't quibble about travel budgets. A few thousand dollars on airfares and hotels is nothing compared to the high-potential products with great margins that can be found along the way.

All over our headquarters are rooms and rooms full of potential product from all over the world. One room will be jammed to the ceiling with lamps, another with memory albums, yet another with silk flowers. The items change as the year moves along; Christmas ornaments, for example, come in November of the *previous* year. We study them and place our orders by February. Meanwhile, garden items arrive in May of the previous year, and the ordering is done by July for the coming spring. It is an ever-changing parade of merchandise to consider.

Retail is a moving target. You cannot "can" this business. You have to stay agile on your feet, always ready to adjust.

T. Boone Pickens Jr., the colorful Texas oilman, once said in a speech at George Washington University, "Be willing to make decisions. That's the most important quality in a good leader. Don't fall victim to what I call the 'ready-aim-aim-aim-aim syndrome.' You must be willing to fire."

My equivalent to that is: A good plan in action is better than a perfect plan on paper. You can analyze until you paralyze.

In our once-a-month buyers meeting, we don't waste time second-guessing one another's choices. Instead, I'll talk about big-picture trends, such as which categories seem to be growing and which are pulling back a bit. At the time of this writing, fountains seem to be waning, while table runners and throw pillows are surging. So one needs to be trimmed back while the others receive more attention.

Or I may do a little training session on how to negotiate overseas, how other cultures negotiate differently than Americans do.

By the end of the day, more than a few of the buyers will be back out in the real world, touching, feeling, looking, checking stock levels, asking questions. On the special items (not year-round), I ask them to do two counts during the season: once in the early going, to make sure we've bought enough, and then a second time in the late innings, just before the product goes on a half-price sale. This will tell us whether we bought too much.

If you knew the right day and whom to look for, you might see five buyers over in Store Number 2 all counting the thousands of Christmas items we carry. One would be focusing on ornaments and table pieces, while another would be tallying nativity scenes and miniatures. By the end of the process, they would know infinitely more than they ever could have learned back at their desks staring at computer printouts.

As you can tell, I place great confidence in these people. They're good at what they do, and I back them 100 percent. That's one of my management principles: Look for chances to go to bat for your people.

Recently one of our young buyers made a decision that disappointed a certain salesman. He had an intriguing product to offer, but his price was too high for us to make the numbers work. So our buyer said no thank you.

The salesman was irritated. In reporting to his supervisor by e-mail, the man lost his cool and wrote: "Maybe you should try to contact her boss. As stated previously: She might be the worst buyer that I have ever met, and seems to have the intelligence of a dockworker . . ."

Well—that e-mail got forwarded along until it inadvertently ended up in our offices! That's the danger with e-mail, as everyone knows; it so easily gets into the wrong hands.

What an insult this was, both to the young woman (who in fact has made a number of very bright moves for us) and to dockworkers in general.

When this hit my desk, it didn't take me longer than fifteen minutes to send out the word across the organization that Hobby Lobby would never again buy from this man. Not one dime's worth of product. I don't care what kind of a hot deal he comes up with. His days of selling to our company are finished.

As I said: Stand up for your people. They will recognize that you value them, and they'll return the favor.

LISTEN AND ADJUST

One of my recurring speeches to our corporate leaders and vice presidents has two points:

1. Take care of your people.
2. Listen to your people.

We sometimes say that the store managers are king. They, along with their staffs, are the ones who make it happen. The rest of us don't bring any money in the door. Nothing really happens until merchandise is sold at the store level.

So it's important for all the rest of us to listen carefully to what the store managers are saying. Everybody at the top levels in the home office knows we have to work together for the benefit of the stores. I really don't have time for big egos around here. They don't last long. We all need to be focused on the stores, not our executive privileges.

> I REALLY DON'T HAVE TIME FOR BIG EGOS
> AROUND HERE. THEY DON'T LAST LONG.
> WE ALL NEED TO BE FOCUSED ON THE
> STORES, NOT OUR EXECUTIVE PRIVILEGES.

John Criner, who opened our Enid, Oklahoma, store back in 1983 and is still there today, was commenting recently about the early days, when all the store managers could fit around one conference table. He still remembers my stock question that came near the end of every agenda: "How can we improve this company?"

John said, "It was a time for us to dream together, to imagine what Hobby Lobby could become. You'd go around the table every meeting and make every one of us give a response. In fact, we managers started preparing ahead of time, because we knew we'd have to be ready to say something to that question." Out of this exercise came many good ideas.

When you're in leadership, you have to give up some of your authority in order to make people's jobs a fun experience. If they don't feel empowered, they're going to dread coming to work in the morning. They need a certain degree of freedom in order to feel that they're making a difference.

I remember going to a craft show years ago and watching the grand entrance of a man who had been recently featured on the trade magazine covers as "Mr. Craft." He swept through the aisles with an entourage of perhaps a dozen underlings. Clearly, he decided everything; they were just along for the effect. He generated a lot of buzz on the exhibit floor by placing an order for forty-two trailerloads of a single product. Wow! Everyone was impressed.

Today that man is out of the business. When you concentrate authority in a single set of hands, it raises the possibility of making big blunders. Far better to spread out the say-so, and grow your people as a result.

Our real estate department, for example, has tremendous latitude in choosing and leasing properties. When our director comes to me with a deal, I almost always say yes; because he's done his homework, he has the numbers to back up his recommendation—and we're ready to go. He's already calculated how good the location is, how much "TI money" (tenant improvement) we're going to need, and all the rest. He's been through the various demographics—things such as:

— Is there enough population? We need a pool of at least 50,000 people who are close enough to shop conveniently at our store.

— How strong are the retail sales *in that area*? Bedroom suburbs, for example, may have lots of people, but if the residents do all their shopping in the metropolitan area next door, that doesn't help us.

— What are the income levels? While we're not looking for the elite, our potential customers have to at least have some expendable income beyond food, housing, and utilities. As I said, all the goods we sell are, in a sense, optional. You can survive day to day without them.

Having done all this research, often with the help of a market analysis agency, we're ready to make decisions. We like to say that the ball is never in our court on a real estate lease. We're always sitting around waiting on the other party; they're never waiting on us to make up our minds.

Once we sign the paperwork and get the construction work done (lighting, painting, etc.), we can open up a new store in two weeks flat. We've done it enough times now that we know how to go from bare floor to a full Hobby Lobby panorama in fourteen days.

That means bringing in ten to twelve truckloads of fixtures alone. Right behind that come around thirty-seven truckloads of merchandise. The job list is detailed right down to who's going to make sure the mats are in place for wiping your feet. Each district manager has a list of people from the stores in that district who are good at store setup. They come together to make it happen in a given city, then go back to their regular jobs. They know exactly what they're to do. It's not a committee thing; it's an exercise in action to reach the goal.

FREEDOM AT THE STORE LEVEL

On the one hand, I suppose you could say Hobby Lobby *limits* the freedom of the store manager when it comes to choosing product. Occasionally, an applicant will say to us, "Well, if I don't get to be a buyer for my store, and I don't get to determine sales, it sounds like all you want me to do is unlock the doors in the morning."

No, that's not the full picture. The store manager and staff have great freedom in displaying the product once it arrives. No plan-o-grams tie their hands, as already explained. They can use their creativity in attracting the customers' attention.

Store managers also get to choose their people. They get to set wages and hand out raises. They get to manage the training and development of their people. They get to focus on actual retailing.

I expect them to use their common sense—not like the TG&Y store I walked into one day years ago when I was a young district co-manager. The safe didn't work, I found out. The store manager was hiding cash up above the back-room ceiling tiles as a result!

"What's the deal?" I asked.

"My budget this month for maintenance and repairs is only $50," he answered.

"For heaven's sake, get the safe fixed!" I ordered. I mean, expense control is important, but this was ridiculous.

In my schedule these days, I make it a point to visit every new Hobby Lobby store. When I do, I usually ask the manager how he or she likes the job, especially compared to where he or she worked before. What is the biggest difference? What has been the biggest surprise?

Nine times out of ten, this is what I hear: "You know, Hobby Lobby is like what that other company was when I loved it twenty years ago—before it got all complex and bogged down. I used to enjoy retail—and now I'm back to how it felt in the beginning. This is fun."

People want to sense that they're making headway, getting something accomplished, and they want to be able to use their heads along the way. They don't want to be cogs in the middle of a gigantic machine. They want flexibility but not anarchy. As we create an environment of creativity that leads to achievement, the workforce is happier, and the customer is better served—which was the point all along.

PART THREE

THE PEOPLE FACTOR

CHAPTER 9

LEADING BY EXAMPLE

Early in my working life at another retailer, before I started Hobby Lobby, I succeeded a store manager who had been stealing from the company. Everybody in the store knew it, and when the district manager found out, he justifiably fired the guy. As a young twenty-four-year-old, I was sent to that store to set a new and better tone.

The curious thing was this: Within six months, I had to dismiss seven employees—about half the workforce—for stealing! The infection of taking what you wanted had spread in all directions. The staff had gotten their cues from the previous manager, so he was not an isolated case. We had multiple problems to straighten out.

Leaders in business—and anywhere else, for that matter—are watched every day to see what kind of character they possess. America has had a fair number of corporate embarrassments recently, from Enron to Tyco to insider trading. The 1990s, it seems, was a greedy decade. The stock market was soaring, everybody wanted to post good numbers, and there was a lot of pressure on executives to cut corners. While many of them stood firm, some yielded and got caught.

We at Hobby Lobby had a good decade, with profits rising 1,271 percent from 1990 to 1999. But as far as I know, we did it with integrity. I can't imagine running a business any other way. The idea of making a promise to someone and not following through with it is just not acceptable. The old Quakers used to have a saying: "His word is his bond." In other words, if he says something, you don't need to ask for a bond or a security deposit or anything else; he's a Quaker, and that means he'll do it, come what may. I try to run my business in the same manner.

It's all part of our corporate commitment to follow biblical principles in everything we do. Some businesspeople think that's a noble claim but that it ties one hand behind your back. I disagree. Nothing taught in the Bible is harmful to business. Doing things God's way pays dividends—maybe not immediately, but in the long run.

The Bible talks openly, for example, about giving customers the full quantity of what they're paying for.[1] It says you shouldn't play money games with your creditors.[2] These are sound, ethical business practices for today.

LESSONS LEARNED EARLY

I feel strongly about these things, I suppose, because I grew up watching my parents live out their faith in clear, observable ways. They believed, for example, that 10 percent (a tithe) of all income should be given to God's work. They applied that not only to their meager salary as small-town ministers, but even to gifts-in-kind.

I mentioned in chapter 1 of this book that parishioners

would regularly try to help out our large family by bringing us fresh produce. My father would go to the trouble of calculating the grocery store value of those beans, tomatoes, or strawberries—and then put 10 percent of that figure in cash into the offering plate. If my mother was given a hand-me-down dress by some woman in the church, she would go through the same exercise, giving back to God a tithe of what she felt the dress was worth.

After I got married and left home at the age of nineteen, my mother came across some box cutters and glass cutters that had wandered home in my pockets from my job at McClellan's five-and-dime. I hadn't meant to steal them; I just hadn't always checked my jeans when leaving the store.

My mother didn't want to make a big thing about this, and she didn't want to embarrass me to the store manager, Mr. Tyler. But she wasn't going to keep the tools or throw them away. So she put them in a little bag, went down to McClellan's, and left them on a counter for one of the staff to find. Only afterward did she tell me what she had done.

That's the kind of integrity I was taught. It's the way I still try to live. People have asked me, "What's the toughest ethical decision you've ever had to make as a businessman?" I don't know what to say, because in my mind things are usually pretty black and white. If we know something's wrong, we don't do it. We on the executive team at Hobby Lobby are of one mind on this. We have total freedom to challenge one another to live up to the biblical standards we espouse.

PLAYING IT STRAIGHT

For example, we routinely report back to the vendors on "longages" in their shipments—not just shortages. If we order 100 cases of something, and the truck delivers only 95, naturally we and every other business will speak up about that shortage. But if for some reason we receive 105 cases, we point that out too.

I've called owners of companies to say, "Hey, we just got your shipment, but you sent us more than what the invoice says." They can hardly believe their ears. "Nobody has ever done this before!" they tell me. Well, we do, because it's right.

We have a strict policy on fairness with vendors. On the wall of our front lobby, where salespeople can see it every time they come to our home office, is the following sign:

NOTICE TO VENDORS

It is Hobby Lobby policy that employees or owners will not receive any gifts of any value from vendors.

Except for rare occasions, employees will not accept dinner engagements, as they will be with their families during the evening.

Hobby Lobby owners and buyers will pay their share of lunches. Any gift received by anyone will be returned to the sender.

Any violation of this policy will jeopardize the relationship between Hobby Lobby Stores, Inc. and the vendor.

We thank you in advance for your cooperation.
                                                    David Green

---

My point here is that favors and kickbacks are not even to be considered. If a vendor has to slide something extra under the table to a buyer, it inevitably drives up the vendor's price on the product, which can only hurt the buyer's company. I'm told that one-third of all corporate failures are related not to external factors but to *internal* corruption. I don't ever want that to happen at Hobby Lobby.

When it comes to paying taxes, we intend to pay our fair share according to the law. As you can well imagine, in a business this size there are hundreds of possible shortcuts. Some of them the IRS would probably never be able to find. But we would know, and so would God.

IN A BUSINESS THIS SIZE THERE ARE HUNDREDS OF POSSIBLE SHORTCUTS. SOME OF THEM THE IRS WOULD PROBABLY NEVER BE ABLE TO FIND. BUT WE WOULD KNOW, AND SO WOULD GOD.

We have been audited several times, with tax agents spending weeks and weeks on our premises. I can't claim they've always agreed with us on every little point; I remember once, for example, when they said, "Well, you have to include in your cost of goods the cost of your overseas buying trips." With picky little stuff like that, we changed to do what they asked. But we've never knowingly tried to dodge a legitimate tax rule.

When we organized a buying office in a certain country, we made it known at the outset that Hobby Lobby would be paying its full share of taxes. The national employees we had hired were very good people, but they still could hardly believe this particular policy. "Nobody pays full taxes in this country!" they explained. "If you do, your money just goes into the pockets of corrupt politicians."

"Well," I replied, "that's not my problem to solve. We're going to do what the law says, regardless." They shook their heads in wonderment.

After we had filed a few tax returns, the country's tax authority stopped by to audit us. They came to a strange conclusion. "You're paying more taxes than some large corporations," they declared. "You shouldn't be doing this."

When I heard the story, I asked myself, *Now why would a tax agent say something like that?*

I finally figured out the angle. If we started cutting corners like everyone else, they would have grounds to say, "You're cheating the government. We're going to have to take you to court—unless you want to, uh . . ." and the invitation to bribery would have been underway.

I told our employees later, "Do you see how this kind of behavior is hurting your country? No wonder the roads aren't being fixed, the schools aren't being improved, and all the rest. Too much money is being diverted from what the people actually need."

Over the long haul, this particular office has proved to be successful for our company. I personally think it has something to do with operating with integrity, despite the prevailing climate.

On the other side of the coin, we're not going to pay *more* than our fair share of taxes and duties either. I read once where Procter & Gamble shut down an entire plant in West Africa for four months rather than pay a $5,000 bribe to a customs official who was holding up an incoming shipment of raw material. Good for them. I'd do the same thing if faced with a similar demand. Not that we couldn't afford the bribe money, but simply because it's wrong.

HOW TO GET FIRED AT HOBBY LOBBY

We insist on integrity at all levels of the organization. Two of the things that will get someone fired immediately are (1) theft and (2) misconduct of a sexual nature. In those two situations, there are no second chances. One strike and you're out.

Pretty close to these would be giving false information. I couldn't handle dealing with an employee, at whatever level, who was not truthful on a report or in a conversation. It's nearly impossible to make good decisions in a business if you're relying on skewed data.

Abraham Lincoln once gave a lecture to fellow lawyers in which he said, "Resolve to be honest at all events; and if in your own judgment you cannot be an honest lawyer, resolve to be honest without being a lawyer. Choose some other occupation, rather than one in the choosing of which you do, in advance, consent to be a knave [scoundrel]."[3] I will resist the urge to make a comment about some of today's lawyers, but I will say that Lincoln's advice is pretty good for retailers too.

On the other hand, I hope we've never fired anybody for lack of knowledge. We spend a lot of time and effort teaching our new store managers how to do their jobs. There's a policy book to guide them. We also encourage them to ask questions of their district manager, or call a more experienced manager in the next city. In spite of our many efforts to simplify store management, it is still a complicated task, and we try our best to help them learn.

Education is one thing; application, however, is another. We have a lot of patience for the first, not so much for the second. If you know what you're supposed to be doing but you aren't applying yourself to the task, that's a different story.

Over the years we have learned that it's very difficult to jack up a person's application level for more than a few months. You can prod and encourage and motivate and even warn people that they need to get moving. But if the core values of hard work and follow-through are not within them, the results of outside prodding usually don't last.

We try to go the second mile, even if deep inside we fear that the chances of success are slim to none. We say things like, "Let me go over this one more time: Hobby Lobby expects your store to be such-and-such-and-such. Let's make it happen, okay?!" Once in a while we see genuine and lasting improvement. More often, it's time for this person to go work somewhere else.

CHARACTER FIRST

A few years ago we came across a character program that we've implemented company-wide. The curriculum company mainly markets to schools, but we decided it was good for our 16,000 employees too.

Once a month, a specific character trait is emphasized in department meetings at headquarters and all across the chain: honesty, for example, or thriftiness, self-control, or initiative. The total list comes to forty-nine traits, which means we move through them all in about a four-year period. In this way we set the tone for the kind of company we want to be.

We also pay attention to speech. I think people expect me, as the CEO, to express myself in respectful terms. For our employees, we don't have firm rules about this, but we have posted a sign at the various entrances to our warehouse that says the following:

Language is the expression of thought. Every time you speak, your mind is on parade. Keep it clean.

Another message is sent by the presence of a full-time paid chaplain at our Oklahoma City office. Dianna Bradley is a marvelous woman with a counseling background who helps employees work through personal issues; everything from marital stress to chemical dependence to worries about children. She also organizes voluntary Bible studies throughout the building, where small groups of people get together before work or on their lunch hour to read Scripture and apply it to their lives.

The rules state that you may not go to the chaplain for any kind of *work-related* problem. If you think your boss is being unfair or taking advantage of you, you have to process that directly with the boss or the boss's immediate supervisor. But for personal, non-work matters, Dianna is more than willing and able to assist you, pointing out how God's Word can give you guidance.

A popular thirteen-week class these days is entitled "Financial Peace," using resources by author Dave Ramsey. It meets once a week for a two-hour session, helping employees gain control of spending patterns, manage debt, and build for a stable future. As the course moves along, surprised students have joyfully reported, "Wow, I actually have money left at the end of a pay period now!"

When asked what her job is, Dianna usually smiles and says, "I get paid to love people." More than once an employee with no religious affiliation has experienced a death in the family and has asked her to conduct the funeral.

One employee came to her and said, "My father is very sick—in fact, he probably won't last much longer. Would you go and see him?" Dianna said sure. The only complication was that the man lived in a small town off in a corner of our state, far from Oklahoma City. It was hardly practical for her to make such a trip.

She didn't drop the matter, however. She began making calls until she found a local pastor who she felt confident would handle the situation well. "Would you be willing to go and see this gentleman on my behalf?" she asked.

The pastor agreed. He called Dianna back the next week, however, to report that the elderly man had been quite unreceptive; he most definitely did *not* want the attention of a minister. Dianna replied, "Well, thank you for making the attempt."

That was the end of things—until a year later. Then came an update: The pastor, despite the first rebuff, had continued to drop by occasionally and see how the man was doing. His health stabilized after all, and in time he softened his attitude. Then, just recently, he made his personal peace with God.

Some may think it strange that a commercial retail company would have a chaplaincy. No more strange than the U.S. Army having chaplains—or, for that matter, the U.S. Congress. We want to give our employees every kind of assistance we can in becoming whole people. It's all part of building an organization of excellence and integrity.

CHAPTER 10

TAKING CARE OF FAMILIES

It was a rainy February night, and I, a young store manager, was bone-tired as I finally left the TG&Y on Britton Road in Oklahoma City at 9:50 P.M. The store had closed at nine o'clock, but it had taken me this long to leave because one department head hadn't finished writing her order, and I couldn't leave until it was transmitted to the warehouse. Finally, another day in the life of a store manager came to an end.

I hunched my shoulders as I ran through the rain to my car for the fifteen-minute drive home to our little 900-square-foot bungalow on Eighty-seventh Street. Dashing inside, I was greeted by Barbara as I hung up my coat and slumped down at the kitchen table. "How was your day, sweetheart?" she asked quietly as she began fixing a little snack.

"Well, okay, I guess," I replied. "Cynthia called in sick, and a couple of customers got upset because we ran out of some stuff we'd advertised. But we made it through."

She gave a weak smile, then sat down across from me. "Mart really wanted to show you the picture he drew in kindergarten today, but I just couldn't let him stay up this late. He made me promise you'd see it anyway—it's taped onto his bedroom door."

I sighed. Tomorrow night I'd have to work late again. But the night after that, I'd finally get to spend some time with our kids. *Is this the way things have to be in order to make a decent living?* I asked myself.

AGAINST THE TIDE

The memory of a thousand nights like that dug a deep groove into my consciousness, so when it came to Hobby Lobby, I made a bold decision: We would close at 8:00 P.M. I knew I was going against the tide of American retail. I knew the last hour of the day is one of the most profitable, and my competitors would definitely stay open to pick up the sales I'd be missing. (Since then, retail hours have gotten even longer, with some drugstores and mass merchandisers staying open till eleven, midnight, or even around the clock.)

But I couldn't get away from the human toll that such a schedule extracts. If I could give my store managers and floor staff just one more hour to be home—maybe to put their kids to bed—it would be a positive thing. If I could somehow reduce the stress on family life and help my employees be more balanced, I'd rather do that than bring in a little extra profit.

I know this is contrary to what the rest of the retail industry considers "smart business." I don't see anybody else in the field following my lead. But I still believe in it. We shut down at eight o'clock, except for a few nights during the Christmas season. We don't run any of those "midnight madness" sales. I think we have a happier workforce as a result.

> WE DON'T RUN ANY OF THOSE
> "MIDNIGHT MADNESS" SALES. I THINK WE
> HAVE A HAPPIER WORKFORCE AS A RESULT.

And interestingly, we've noticed our customer base adjusting to our schedule. Whereas other stores say the foot traffic picks up around eight o'clock, we see our evening crowd starting to hit the doors around seven o'clock! They know they've got only an hour to shop at Hobby Lobby, so they put us first on their list after dinner.

WHAT ABOUT SUNDAY?

It wasn't until 1998 that we got around to facing an even larger, more controversial question: Should we be open on Sundays? Obviously, Sunday is a very good business day in America. We looked at our sales reports and noted, at that time, we were taking in $100 million a year on Sundays. Our sales-per-hour were highest on that day of any in the week. To rock that boat would be a serious disruption.

But again, I thought back to my earlier days as a store manager. I remembered how, even if I would schedule myself not to work on a Sunday, I was still never truly "off." I'd be getting ready to go to church, and I would be thinking, *I wonder if everything got opened all right. Did everybody show up for work the way they were supposed to? Did all the sale signs get put up on the correct items? Will the staff stay alert for any pilferage?*

I knew that every store manager across the Hobby

Lobby chain was still doing the same thing. Whenever the store doors are open, he or she is carrying the responsibility, whether on the premises or not. The manager is the captain of the ship.

Plus, those employees who wanted to attend church at the normal hour on Sunday morning often couldn't. Our workforce, like any company's, included a fair percentage of churchgoers, and the demands of our schedule were interfering with their spiritual lives. Was this right from a company whose owners were active Christians themselves?

The value of having a "day of rest" each week is centuries old, and is not exclusively Christian. The Jewish faith proclaims the same thing, although on Saturday; the Muslims, on Friday. Apparently there is a rhythm built into the created order—work no more than six days, then take one off—that shouldn't be ignored. The French Revolution tried to gain efficiency (and knock religion) by installing a ten-day "week" from 1793 to 1805; it just didn't work. The Bolsheviks tried again as soon as they took over Russia in 1917. "Later, for 11 years starting in 1929," says one authority, "Stalin imposed first five-day and then six-day weeks on the Soviet Union. The elimination of Sunday, with its strong religious association, was one purpose of his experiments. They all failed, abjectly."[1]

I didn't have the courage—or faith—to shut down on Sunday all at once, so I took a baby step instead. "Let's try this out in one state—say, Nebraska," I told our team. Of course, we had only three stores in Nebraska!

We gave the three managers instructions to close. They could hardly believe we were serious. One was so committed to the company's well-being that he couldn't help worrying aloud about what would happen to our profits.

We pressed ahead. We put a modest sign in the windows:

> *Closed Sundays to Allow Employees*
> *Time for Family & Worship*

As you might expect, sales numbers immediately took a dip.

The *Omaha World-Herald* quickly noticed and starting working on a story. After all, we were already one of their advertisers. One of the business reporters telephoned Bill Hane, our advertising director, to ask, "What's the deal here? What are you doing?"

Bill explained that we felt this was the right thing to do for our employees. He also said this was in line with the Christian convictions of the owners about respecting one day a week. Then he added, "You know, if everything works out, we're going to close all the stores, not just Nebraska."

When I read that in the paper, something nudged me on the inside. It was as if God was saying to my spirit, *Oh . . . so if you're blessed, you're going to be obedient? But if the numbers don't work out for you, then maybe not?*

I knew that wasn't right. I called Bill immediately and said, "If any other reporters ask, tell them we're closing all the stores on Sunday, period. It's a done deal."

What I didn't know at the time was that my bankers were nervous because we owed them a lot of money. They didn't say anything to me, but they told me later that they certainly talked among themselves, wondering if their loans were endangered.

Well, as it turned out, a curious thing happened in Nebraska. Very soon the sales volumes began rebounding to their previous levels, and kept climbing. We added Alabama and Arkansas to the policy. By the next year we phased in Kansas, Missouri, Oklahoma, and Colorado. By Mother's Day of 2000, when we closed all the Texas stores, we had completed the list.

Other newspapers carried the story. Our hometown paper, the *Daily Oklahoman*, said on the editorial page, "In an age of elastic morals and 'no controlling legal authority,' holding to one's beliefs stands out. Retailers voluntarily closing on the Sabbath will probably remain as rare as ham on a Passover plate, but we commend those who make the sacrifice."

Rare is correct; the only other national retailer I know to do this is Chick-fil-A, the Atlanta-based fast-service food chain with 1,125 stores across 37 states. Its founder and chairman, S. Truett Cathy, holds the same convictions I do. But neither one of us is especially worried about being in the majority.

Hobby Lobby's corporate earnings during this transition showed greater sales but less profit. Once we got fully switched, however, the next year (2001) showed the highest percentage of profit in our history. Once we did what we knew we were supposed to do, profits took off.

Meanwhile, the response from employees has been ecstatic. The staff at our Baton Rouge, Louisiana, store sent me a group letter signed by everyone, saying, "It is with heartfelt thanks that we, the associates of #147, join the thousands of other associates across the states in applauding our corporate leaders for taking the bold step in Sunday closings. We know this is a positive for Hobby Lobby and pray that other retailers will join us in bringing back those things that are important in our lives."

Well, that prayer hasn't yet been answered. In fact, in

response to our window sign, our main competitor in the home-and-craft industry put up a sign for a while that said, "Open on Sunday for the Convenience of Our Customers." That's all right; they certainly have a right to run their business as they choose. I just continue to believe that if God is able to make 90 percent of a tithing person's salary go further than 100 percent, he is able to make six days better than seven.

> I JUST CONTINUE TO BELIEVE THAT IF GOD IS ABLE TO MAKE 90 PERCENT OF A TITHING PERSON'S SALARY GO FURTHER THAN 100 PERCENT, HE IS ABLE TO MAKE SIX DAYS BETTER THAN SEVEN.

Besides, isn't it enough to be open sixty-six hours a week? That's our schedule at Hobby Lobby. Hardly any of our customers work sixty-six hours a week. They have the time to stop by and pick up what they want during the hours we're open. We feel that we've struck a reasonable balance between serving our customers—which is vitally important in retail—and taking care of our families.

A few years ago, the in-flight magazine of United Air Lines carried an interesting article by a fairly secular Jewish woman, Nan Chase, about how she and her entrepreneur husband, Saul, had revived their lives and their home (with three adolescent children) by taking a "day of rest." With eloquence she wrote, "If someone told you there was a way to stop the onslaught of everyday obligations, improve your social life, keep the house clean, revive your tired marriage, elevate spiritual awareness, and improve productivity at work—all overnight and without cost—you'd probably say the claim was absurd. I certainly did. But . . . I've discovered that adherence to a seemingly arcane set of Sabbath rules yields a precious gift." Her article then went on to give the details.[2]

One of the benefits we never anticipated in the beginning has been the quality of retail people who apply to work for a six-day-a-week company. Over the last few years, we've been amazed to see how many top-notch, family-oriented, solid, productive managers and other employees want to leave where they are and come work for Hobby Lobby. We never even thought about that ripple effect!

LIFE IS MORE THAN WORK

It's interesting to listen to some of these applicants. They tell about being lectured in the past: "This company is your life. You take care of business here, and the business will take care of your family." As a result, one of America's major dis-counters is notorious for its dreadfully high divorce rate among managers.

I used to work for a fellow like that. I can still hear him saying, "David, your kids are going to grow up and leave you sooner or later. But you'll always have your job here—as long as you give it 120 percent. Make sure this place is okay, and everything else will be okay."

Well, the facts are that *nobody* has a job at that company today; it's out of business. And more tragically, the man who was giving me the big pitch ended up committing suicide.

I tell everyone at Hobby Lobby that this company is

not their priority in life. Their family is more important than this business. I'm not looking for people who will work seventy or eighty hours a week. If a manager tells me he's so committed to running a perfect store that he's putting in those kind of hours, I tell him to leave. Go somewhere else. I don't care if I'm making all the money in the world from his store—if that's what it takes, I'm not interested.

As a matter of fact, that is *not* what it takes. I know from personal experience. If you're willing to delegate, and you're organized, you don't have to burn the midnight oil very often. What are the three most important things about managing a store? Organization, organization, and organization.

To the manager who says he needs to work an extra fifteen hours each week to keep his store shipshape, I respond: "Wait a minute. You've got fifty employees each working forty hours a week, right? That's 2,000 hours of effort. Are you telling me that if you could just pull together 2,015 hours of effort, it would make a huge difference? I don't buy that.

"The problem is not hours; the problem is your organization. The football coach doesn't get out onto the field to win games. Instead he gets the right people in the right places doing the right things. Once he trains and motivates properly, the scoreboard takes care of itself.

"If you hire the right people and train them properly so that you get just 10 percent more productivity, you will have gained the equivalent of two hundred more hours—not just fifteen."

Once I got chewed out by my supervisor after he noticed I wasn't working long hours. "Don't make it look so easy, David," he said. "You're confusing the other managers."

Years ago, an associate and I were working together to open a new 80,000-square-foot store, one of TG&Y's family centers. We left every night by five or five-thirty. The supervisor would come by in the evening to see how the project was coming along, and we'd be closed! He'd stop by on Sunday, and again the place would be locked up.

He couldn't figure out what was going on, or *not* going on. A normal store opening in that chain required a layout crew of some twenty people. We had used our own employees plus just three extras from other stores. In the end, the store opened on time and for the least amount of expense per square foot they had ever seen.

It's not about working harder. It's about working smarter—using your common sense to organize.

I'm not saying I don't work long hours in crunch times. I do, and I expect others to do the same. Christmastime can be a tough two or three weeks in a store. You bear down and do what you have to do. You don't cry about it; you just get through it.

If December sales have been absolutely crazy, you may have to restock on Sunday in order to get ready for Monday. Occasionally I'll get a letter from an employee complaining, "Hey, my boss made me work last Sunday. I thought you said God told you not to do that." I probably should write back and say, "From what I've learned from your supervisors, this was a rare, exceptional case. We never gave an ironclad promise that *no one* would ever have to work a Sunday. But think about it: Isn't it nice that you've had forty-nine or fifty Sundays off over the past year? Wouldn't that be a reason to say thank you?"

When you take good care of your people in retail, they stay happier. Their families stay happier. The whole company runs more smoothly. It's a win-win-win situation.

> **WHEN YOU TAKE GOOD CARE OF YOUR PEOPLE IN RETAIL, THEY STAY HAPPIER. THEIR FAMILIES STAY HAPPIER. THE WHOLE COMPANY RUNS MORE SMOOTHLY. IT'S A WIN-WIN-WIN SITUATION.**

If a manager asks for a transfer due to some family reason, we do our best to accommodate. If, for example, a manager in Illinois says, "My elderly parents down in Texas are not doing very well—is there any chance I could get closer to them?" we will search diligently to find an appropriate opening in Texas. Yes, this can be expensive for the company. But people are more important than profits.

As a result, we tend to keep our people for a long time. Naturally, we're always going to be losing some people, from those who view retail as simply a start-up position, to those whose spouse got transferred somewhere, to those who simply don't like the work once they begin. But for us to hold on to a strong part of our workforce from one year to the next is a great benefit.

As one trade reporter wrote, "Hobby Lobby must be a good place to work, because the employee turnover rate is very low." That rate, in fact, has continued to go down as we've been able to raise wages and increase benefits. We have warehouse people who have been pulling stock for us for five, ten, and even fifteen years.

In the year 2000, the United Steelworkers of America tried to organize our warehouse as a union shop. After all their efforts to convince employees to join, they lost the election in a landslide, 17 percent *yes* to 83 percent *no*. The Teamsters also came around trying to get a foothold. They couldn't drum up enough interest even to hold an election.

I'm not criticizing the labor movement in an overall sense. I just believe we're already voluntarily doing for our workforce what labor unions seek to achieve.

We can't claim to have built heaven on earth, where there are no unhappy employees. We have to guide our managers to achieve the right balance between corporate achievement and employee contentment. Sometimes a manager will tilt a little too much in one direction or the opposite. We have to find the proper medium.

But deep down, I don't think it's healthy to view business and family life as a tug-of-war. Paying attention to family life is a way to build stronger business through a stable organization.

THE WIDER VIEW

I even believe in looking out for the good of families in the communities we serve, beyond the names on our own payroll.

Back in 2001, we ran into a difficult situation where the neighborhood of one of our stores in a certain city began to deteriorate rapidly. The drug traffickers moved in, and things really began falling apart. Soon it wasn't safe for our employees—or our customers—to keep coming to the store. What were we going to do?

We finally made the troubling decision that we would need to relocate the store to another part of the city.

The only trouble was, we had ten years yet to go on our lease for this 55,000-square-foot building at $6 a square foot. We were obligated to keep paying the owner $330,000 a year for the life of the lease. That's what you call "paying for a dead horse." A very expensive horse.

Suddenly, another business came along to rescue us from our dilemma. They would be happy to sign a sublease from us at the same rate, and we could get out from under this financial burden. The only problem: It was for a wholesale liquor outlet.

I thought to myself, "You know, that's just about the last thing this neighborhood needs. It's already got a bunch of problems—they don't need another big provider of alcohol in the community."

We politely declined the offer.

To this day, Hobby Lobby is still shelling out $330,000 a year for that building, which remains vacant. In addition, we face ongoing taxes and insurance. I wish we didn't have to spend that money. If nothing changes, it will cost us more than $3.3 million before the lease runs out. But I'm convinced it's the right thing to do for the families who live nearby.

Without going into a theological or moral discussion about drinking, let me just make a pragmatic point: Here in twenty-first-century America, we have a huge problem with alcohol. I still get weak in the knees whenever I think back to the day when Barbara and I and our baby son Mart (only one year old at the time) were heading west on U.S. Route 62 between Lawton and Altus, Oklahoma, and got side-swiped by a drunk driver. Seat belts weren't mandatory back then, and if the impact had been a few more inches head-on, he would have killed all three of us.

U.S. News & World Report recently reported, in a feature entitled "The Price of Booze," that "alcohol abuse costs American businesses an estimated $134 billion a year."[3] My goodness, that's the equivalent of a hundred Hobby Lobby companies! I know from personal experience that every time some driver under the influence swerves in front of one of our trucks, I seem to end up paying, even if my driver was not at fault. Or far worse than that: Just a couple of months ago, one of our drivers was stopped along the highway tending to a tire that had blown out. A drunk driver came along and killed him.

I just don't want to have anything to do with this menace. A while back, it turned out that our trucks returning from our Colorado stores could have back-hauled Coors Beer to Oklahoma City on a long-term contract that would have netted us $300,000 a year. It was a time when we really could have used the cash.

But again, we said no thank you, preferring to let our trucks come back empty until we could find an alternative. Let somebody else haul the beer and take the responsibility for what people do with it.

Others may disagree with me, and that's all right. I just hope we can agree on the principle of always looking at our business decisions and asking whether they strengthen families or help tear them down.

CHAPTER 11

HIGH EXPECTATIONS

If anyone stopped reading this book after the previous chapter, they may have gone away believing we're a soft and cushy place to collect a paycheck. Well, not entirely. In exchange for our family-friendly policies and practices, we think it's all right to hold employees to high standards of productivity. We're not a happy-time social club.

Instead, as I often say, "We are an above-average company in need of above-average passion for what we do."

GOT YARN?

One of the ways we hold store managers accountable is our monthly random stock checkups. Every store employee in every city knows that sometime during the month the district manager is going to walk through the front door with a list of 100 items out of the 46,000 standing items that are supposed to be on the shelf ready for customers. He or she is going to go around and mark them off, one by one, coming up with a grade at the end.

One month the district manager may be looking for yellow four-inch gift bags, pear-sorbet-scented jar candles, hunter green stencil paint crème, 5 x 8 wirebound sketchbooks, and ninety-six other products from all over the store.

The next month, it will be tabletop fountain pump kits, royal blue half-inch ribbon, berry-red wax crystals for candlemaking, star-shaped cake pans . . .

The third month, it will be lavender clip-on lampshades, citrus green paper napkins (small), 5/16-inch wood dowels, packs of peel-off "wiggle eyes" with lashes, pink yarn . . . Well, you get the idea.

You never know what's going to be in the list of one hundred from month to month.

You also never know when the district manager is going to arrive. One month it may be on the fifth, the next on the nineteenth. One month it may be at 10:00 A.M., the next month at 7:30 P.M. You can't "time" either the content or the hour of your inspection; you just have to be ready at all times.

Why do we do this? Because of this fairly obvious fact of retail: *You can't sell what you don't have available.* If the merchandise is not out there and ready to go, no money is going to land in the till. It's that simple.

And the customer who repeatedly doesn't find what she's looking for is going to migrate to your competitor.

The buyers at the home office take responsibility for deciding *what* Hobby Lobby will stock. The weekly ads take responsibility for drawing customers into the aisles. And the local store has to take equal responsibility for making sure the merchandise is in front of the customers' eyeballs.

All the monthly grades from all over the chain are collected, and these are tabulated as the year moves along. After the December numbers are in, we look at the annual standings from top to bottom—and pay a nice bonus to the top 30 percent of the store managers. At the top end, these bonuses start in the $5,000 range, then $4,500, then $4,000, and so on down to $1,000. In other words, it is definitely worth your while to try to qualify.

Once again, as in the case of the quarterly payroll control bonus mentioned back in chapter 5, if you fail to get this bonus in early January, your spouse is going to let you know about it. That way I don't have to yell and holler at the managers.

This system, I believe, is one of the best ways to keep store managers alert and paying attention to the core work. To earn this bonus, you simply have to be organized. You can't "assume" things are in stock. You have to know what's going on in your store. You have to train your staff to be diligent in their merchandising and weekly inventorying. You have to focus on the reason you're in business, which is to sell product.

Sometimes this stock checkup by a district manager will discover that out-of-stock items are tending to cluster in just one department of a store. The others are doing fine, but one department head isn't paying attention. This person may have a wonderful personality and be a real charmer. But if he isn't sticking his nose into every counter and checking every single item, he's going to be exposed sooner or later.

Even camouflage doesn't work. The department may look fine to the casual eye, with all the peg hooks filled—but not necessarily with all the intended products. A detailed checkup reveals the truth, enabling the district manager to say to the local manager, "You're doing fine in floral and needlework—but you've got a problem in crafts. Better spend some time with that department head."

To quote the old management proverb, "You can't *ex*pect what you don't *in*spect."

Some readers may object, "Yeah, but what if the main warehouse is out of stock on something for a while? Then the store looks bad, and it's not really their fault."

Our warehouse is very diligent when it comes to stocking all the standing items, but if they are out of stock on something and can't ship, all the stores suffer and suffer alike. And at the end of the year, bonuses are awarded "on the curve." The top 30 percent get bonuses, the bottom 70 percent don't. Thus the system is fair after all.

As a matter of fact, the warehouse doesn't stay out of stock on anything for very long. Stores can almost always get what they're being asked to carry. They just have to be on top of their needs.

> A DISTRICT MANAGER IS NOT JUST SOME GUY WHO STOPS BY FOR FUN, BUYS THE STORE MANAGER A CUP OF COFFEE, AND SAYS, "YOUR STORE LOOKS PRETTY." A STORE CAN LOOK "PRETTY"—WITH NOTHING HAPPENING FROM A BUSINESS POINT OF VIEW.

While not having an item on the counter is the major issue here, the monthly checkup also reveals the opposite problem, namely, overstocking. District managers know what the basic levels are supposed to be, and if they see a lot more than that, they flag this as well.

In other words, a district manager is not just some guy who stops by for fun, buys the store manager a cup of coffee, and says, "Your store looks pretty." A store can look "pretty"—with nothing happening from a business point of view.

We believe that by paying attention to details and making sure the customer has every option to buy, the business can prosper. We've built our systems toward that end.

NO SLOPPINESS

During a separate visit in the month, the district manager is looking at a myriad of details that relate to good order. Following are several examples:

— Are the restrooms clean?

— Do the doors have proper signs?

— Have the fire extinguishers been recently checked?

— Are the back doors locked?

— Is new merchandise being displayed within forty-eight hours of arrival?

— Are the manager's office files in order?

— Is the manager's policy book up to date?

— Is the stockroom neat and orderly?

— Is all the clearance merchandise marked down as it should be? (Twice a year we "clean house," gathering all the seasonal and onetime items that have passed their date range and need to be cleared out. The month after these announcements go out to the stores, district managers are checking for follow-through.)

Is Hobby Lobby an "easy place to work"? Not necessarily. Some applicants who are fellow Christians of mine think I'll be all nice and soft and sloppy in order not to hurt anyone's feelings. That's not the case at all. The Bible that I carry says, "Whatever you do, work at it with all your heart, as working for the Lord, not for men" (Colossians 3:23). If anything, the Christian employee ought to be more diligent than anyone, given this spiritual perspective.

Dorothy Sayers, the British writer who inspired C. S. Lewis and a number of others, put her finger on the matter when she wrote:

> The Church's approach to an intelligent carpenter is usually confined to exhorting him not to be drunk and disorderly in his leisure hours, and to come to church on Sundays. What the Church *should* be telling him is this: that the very first demand that his religion makes upon him is that he should make good tables. Church [attendance] by all means, and decent forms of amusement, certainly—but what use is all that if in the very center of his life and occupation he is insulting God with bad carpentry? . . . The only Christian work is a good work well done.[1]

I'm not about to insult God by running a sloppy retail company. I'm determined to do the best job I can. If part of this means telling someone that he or she is not meeting our standards and need to go work somewhere else, I'm quite willing to do so—and have. We want to be the very best workplace for people who are serious about doing a good job. The rest need not apply.

> ## I'M NOT ABOUT TO INSULT GOD BY RUNNING A SLOPPY RETAIL COMPANY.

Fortunately, we've been able to collect a wonderfully responsible team of people over the years. Some are religious, some are not. Regardless, they are people who are glad to show up on time and give a full day's effort. They understand the numerical goals and commit themselves to meet them.

A lot of our best people have come from other retail environments where they were having to work an insane number of hours. Or the company that employed them went out of business—that's happening constantly, it seems. We have a lot of candidates to choose from, and we try to make wise selections.

The interesting thing is, once they arrive at Hobby Lobby and like what they see, they start calling their buddies. This brings us even more good people. (In fact, we pay a small bonus for these referrals, because we've found them to be valuable over the years.)

WHAT ABOUT FAMILY MEMBERS?

As you've noticed by now, a number of Green family members are involved in Hobby Lobby. I hold them to the same performance standards as everyone else. I didn't push any of them to join us in the first place. I said, "If you want to work here, you're welcome—but you'll get only what you earn. This place is like a tree that can bear fruit if it's taken care of. In the final analysis, it doesn't belong to you, or even to Mom and me; it belongs to God. We all have to give it our best attention so that the tree stays strong and healthy for decades to come."

It took me a while as a father to let my three children be in the workplace the way God had made them to be. Steve, for example, is quieter and more thoughtful than I am. He mulls things over. In the early days, I thought I had to "train" Steve in the ways of business. I would come down rather forcefully on him at times.

Eventually, I was praying about all this one day, and the Lord seemed to impress me with this idea: *You're not training him, you're trying to* change *him. What you want Steve to be is not who he is.*

I thought about that, and I saw it was true. I went to my son and said, "Steve, I'm sorry. I've been dead-wrong in how I've related to you here. I need to find out who you really are, and then work with that. We're not all the same."

Things have gone much better since then. Today Steve is our president. He's in the right slot for his temperament.

Darsee, our daughter, started out as a front-desk receptionist. She liked meeting the public; she has a very outgoing personality. Then she moved into being the notions buyer. She hated it! All the paperwork and math just depressed her creative spirit. After several other stops, she landed in her niche at last: creative director. She thrives in the world of design and innovation.

I don't want to paint an overly perfect picture about working with family members. We still have differences of opinion from time to time. If one of them wants to do something I think is unwise, but it's not very expensive, I'll tend to yield. Why? Well, for one thing, I might be wrong! And even if I'm correct, there's a lesson to be learned here; the family member needs to learn what *doesn't* work.

Jeff, my nephew who heads Greco Frame & Supply, had an idea a while back to install a "frame supervisor" in each of the Hobby Lobby districts (groups of fifteen to twenty stores in a geographical area). This person, he felt, could give leadership to the frame departments and really make them flourish.

I said okay, even though in my bones I remembered something from TG&Y days that made me hesitate. With such an "expert" in place, I feared that the store managers would back off when it came to frames and stop taking responsibility. Well, that is more or less what started happening. Before long, we had to abandon the structure.

But I don't fault Jeff for wanting to try this. What he, and we all, learned through this experience was worth the price tag.

On larger proposals that cost big money, however, I've been known to cast a fatherly/CEO veto if I feel negatively about them. And the family has accepted my lead in these cases, without hard feelings. They really are of one heart and mind about our overall purpose.

WHO CAN LIGHT A FIRE?

Even though we have around 16,000 employees overall, we've tried to keep the hiring process simple and direct. Who is willing and able to get the job done for us?

We try to promote from within as much as possible. In fact, I get spooked by big-sounding résumés from outside candidates. If they say they can walk on water and solve all of Hobby Lobby's challenges within six months, I tend to run the other way. I'm looking instead for loyal, long-term people I can trust.

You may be surprised to learn that we're not real big on written job descriptions. Employees know what we expect, but not because we've drafted some long-winded document about it. We've instead looked them in the eye and said verbally, "Here's what you need to do to succeed at Hobby Lobby."

> WE'RE NOT REAL BIG ON WRITTEN JOB DESCRIPTIONS. EMPLOYEES KNOW WHAT WE EXPECT, BUT NOT BECAUSE WE'VE DRAFTED SOME LONG-WINDED DOCUMENT ABOUT IT.

I don't ever want somebody telling me, "Well, that's not in my job description, you know." Whatever needs to get done, we all get after it together. We're a team. If I were to hear the words "I wasn't hired to do that," well . . . I wouldn't hear that from that person more than once.

What I'm looking for in a leader at any level is not somebody with one eye on his job description but rather somebody who can fire up a team. We have former store managers who have risen to become senior vice presidents. Why? Because they showed the ability to motivate people. Their crew was excited to come to work. They built a team that could be effective, month after month.

You can't have that kind of crew if you lack integrity. You can't have that kind of team if you treat them unfairly. You can't post good results if you're personally disorganized.

I've noticed something over the years about quality managers, the kind I call "A" people. When they hire, they inevitably choose other "A" people. The organization benefits as a result.

"B" people, on the other hand, tend to choose "C" people. Why is that? Because down deep inside, they're intimidated by "A" people. So they swing the other direction. They make sure no subordinate of theirs is going to show them up. As a result, the organization is weakened.

The corollary to this is that when "A" people find themselves working for a "B" boss, they start looking for the exit. Something inside them just can't stand to be around mediocrity. Meanwhile, "B" and "C" people working for a "B" boss keep hanging on year after year. After all, it's a paycheck, right?

Finding and nurturing "A" people is incredibly important. And high expectations, oddly enough, have a way of building high morale. People aren't discouraged by the fact that a bar is set high; they rise to meet it. And they feel better about themselves every time they clear it. This is true whether you're unpacking boxes, managing a local store, or running a whole division.

Every business leader talks about growth—well, growth depends on "A" people. If I had all the cash in the world, I would not open one hundred new stores next year. That would require two hundred topflight people (one hundred managers, one hundred co-managers) plus a thousand or two additional quality department heads, and I'm not sure we could find that many that quick. We are determined that our growth will be quality growth, not just an increased number of dots on a map.

In his book *Excellence*, John W. Gardner (a cabinet secretary in the Johnson administration) wrote:

The society which scorns excellence in plumbing because plumbing is a humble activity, and tolerates shoddiness in philosophy because it is an exalted activity, will have neither good plumbing nor good philosophy. Neither its pipes nor its theories will hold water.[2]

I'm for excellence at every level of our company, and I've learned over the years that it doesn't happen without setting clear expectations and then enforcing them. We owe it to ourselves, our coworkers, and, most of all—our customers.

PART FOUR

MORE THAN A HOBBY

CHAPTER 12

THIS IS NOT A "SECULAR" BUSINESS

Barbara and I were at the breakfast table one Christmas morning in the mid-1990s, taking it easy after a big family celebration the night before. All the kids and grandkids had been at our place for our traditional dinner and gift giving. Now the house was quiet, the wrapping paper had been cleaned up, and we were relaxing in a warm holiday mood.

I paged through the morning newspaper, stopping to read a few articles here and there. Eventually I got back to the sports section, and soon only the classifieds were left . . . when an odd question disturbed my consciousness. Why in the December 25th issue did this whole newspaper have nothing to say—not a single paragraph—about the birth of Jesus? There were lots of "Seasons Greetings" and "Happy Holidays," but that was all.

It didn't seem right. Wasn't the arrival of the Baby in Bethlehem the whole origin of *Christ*mas? Then why were they taking up page after page talking about everything from politics to stock-market prospects in the year to come?

Well, I couldn't do anything about the news columns or the editorial page, but I was, after all, an advertiser in this newspaper, as well as more than 250 other papers across the country. Every week I was already paying money to put out my message about the coming week's sale items. Couldn't I spend more of my money to spotlight the eternal importance of Christmas?

A TIME TO BE BOLD

I knew, of course, that some people would say a "secular business" should not get involved in such a thing. But I've never been real fond of the word *secular*. I looked it up in one dictionary that defined it as, among other meanings, "without God." Was that what I wanted Hobby Lobby to be? Not at all.

I began to talk with Barbara and the children about an advertising approach. "I think we need to do something that's more important than commerce," I said. "Nobody else is talking about the real meaning of the holidays that are so significant to us as merchants. We bring in a lot of money thanks to Christmas and Easter. Let's be bold about what the days truly mean."

They agreed with me, and so we prepared a modest ad—only about six inches square—for the next Easter. The following Christmas we ran a half page. Ever since then, it's been a full page in every city where Hobby Lobby operates. You can see the whole gallery of ads on our Web site at www.hobbylobby.com/site3/ministry/message.cfm.

The text of the first Easter ad back in 1997 showed a crown of thorns and said:

For God so loved the world he gave
acceptance
peace
mercy
confidence
purpose
forgiveness
simplicity
hope
relief
comfort
equality
life
his Son.
This Easter, we encourage you to believe in
the love that sent Jesus Christ.
Accept the hope. Accept the joy. Accept the LIFE!

Hobby Lobby Stores Inc.

The next Christmas, we showed a baby in a manger with an oversize hand reaching down. The text read:

When man reaches for God, we call it religion.
When God reaches for man, we call it Christmas.

Through an act of love, greater than our minds can
comprehend,
you have been called by the great heart of God.

He knew you before you were born;
he called you to himself through his Son, Jesus Christ;

and he calls you today,
at this season of celebration,
to know Jesus as Savior and Lord.

You have been called;
how will you respond?

We felt this ad worked so well that we ran it again at Christmas 2002. Otherwise, we have come up with new material each time.

A couple of years into the program, we began adding a toll-free number at the bottom: 1-888-NEED-HIM. This is the number for a twenty-four-hour counseling center in Dallas that helps callers with their spiritual questions. We don't own this organization, and it charges us nothing for its services. But we contribute to its expenses because we believe in what it does.

WHAT PEOPLE THINK

Yes, this kind of thing is daring for a retail company to do. I suppose it isn't "politically correct." I'm not especially worried about that—not when I read the hundreds of letters and e-mails, 99 percent of which are complimentary. Some of the stories will bring tears to your eyes. For instance, people who were alone at Christmas and saw the ad thanked us profusely for inviting them to reach out for spiritual help during their lowest moment. Hundreds if not thousands of people since 1997 have made their peace with God through this inspirational ad campaign.

At the same time, of course, others have taken offense— and told us so. "Are you a business or a church?" the question usually goes. We get a trickle of letters, some from reasonable folks, some downright nasty. Bill Hane, our director of advertising, takes time to answer each one with a personalized reply. And he'll keep the dialogue going as long as the other person wants.

One man called our ad "about the silliest—and sickest—ad I've ever read." He went on to say we were wasting our stockholders' money on such ventures.

Bill wrote a page-and-a-half response that politely recognized the man's complaint. He pointed out that Hobby Lobby, as a privately held, family-owned company, has no outside stockholders. He sent a thought-provoking book, *Mere Christianity* by C. S. Lewis, for the customer's further reflection. In return, Bill got a much calmer acknowledgment.

A businessman in Iowa frowned on "mixing religion with business" and said our ad was a case of "flexing your corporate clout." Bill Hane, after searching his letter for some small point of common ground, replied:

> We join you in celebrating the freedom of expression provided by this great country. . . . It is surely possible to disagree without hatred, and to debate without being called ignorant. It is my faith in this fact and the clear teachings of Jesus Christ that hold me accountable to this civil balance. For this reason I cannot, and you should hope I would not, separate my faith from my business . . .
>
> Thanks very much for taking time to write. Be assured you are appreciated as an individual and as a customer.

This whole assumption on the part of many people that there should be a Jeffersonian "wall of separation" between faith and business is a view I have never accepted. I am who

I am, a merchant who believes and respects Jesus Christ. To say that I should walk out of church on Sunday at noon and then stuff everything I've heard and practiced into a dark closet for the next six days is not realistic, or even desirable. In fact, customers had better *hope* that I treat them according to the moral teachings of my faith!

> THERE IS NO GETTING AROUND THE FACT THAT JESUS OFFENDS SOME PEOPLE. NEVERTHELESS, HE IS TOO IMPORTANT IN MY LIFE FOR ME TO COWER IN FEAR OF MENTIONING HIS NAME.

They don't have to agree with me on all religious matters. They don't have to embrace the same Savior I embrace. But surely there's nothing wrong with my holding him up for public consideration.

One of the most chilling responses to our ads—especially for those of us who live in Oklahoma City—came from an anonymous person who took our Easter ad showing the empty tomb, cut out the opening, and replaced it with the face of Timothy McVeigh (the convicted bomber of the Murrah Federal Building downtown). The person then mailed it to us with a one-sentence note: "This is what you'll get if you keep this up."

Well, there is no getting around the fact that Jesus offends some people. Nevertheless, he is too important in my life for me to cower in fear of mentioning his name. If I'm willing to spend money every other week of the year talking to forty-one million readers about throw pillows, birdhouses, and wicker baskets, I ought to be willing to spend money twice a year talking to the same forty-one million about my Lord.

> **IF I'M WILLING TO SPEND MONEY EVERY OTHER WEEK OF THE YEAR TALKING TO FORTY-ONE MILLION READERS ABOUT THROW PILLOWS, BIRDHOUSES, AND WICKER BASKETS, I OUGHT TO BE WILLING TO SPEND MONEY TWICE A YEAR TALKING TO THE SAME FORTY-ONE MILLION ABOUT MY LORD.**

What they choose to do with my advertising message is their free choice. Even some of my own employees see things differently, I'm sure; as I've said before, we have no Christian requirement to work at Hobby Lobby. That would be illegal, in fact. We simply set a positive environment that happens to be based on biblical principles, and let people draw their own conclusions.

I can't think of any employee who has ever said he or she felt pressured toward Christianity by the workplace atmosphere. Neither have I ever heard an employee say he or she wished we wouldn't run the message ads. Nobody has said, "You're going to scare off certain customers." They accept the fact that we are not a "secular" employer, and they've known this from their first day on the job. Spiritual topics are not taboo in this workplace. We talk about them openly.

Meanwhile, the general public sees us as distinctly different from the prevailing winds of holiday times in America, especially Christmas. They see schools and other institutions tiptoeing around to avoid the mention of whose birthday it is. They read about the legal wrangling over whether a nativity display can appear in the city park. Even a Christmas tree is offensive in some quarters, it seems.

And then—in the midst of all this posturing—here comes a business (not a church) with a full-page ad about the central point of the holiday. "I would expect this from a clergyman," they say to themselves, "but why would a *merchant* do this? Why would a retail store spend millions of dollars all over the country this way? They must really believe in something."

Yes, we do.

A DIFFERENT TONE

Throughout this book, I've already mentioned several other things that illustrate the belief system of Hobby Lobby: the music we play in our stores, the work of the headquarters chaplain, the "Character First" program for all employees, the allowance for a day of worship.

Recently, we provided to all officers and buyers a free copy of the best-selling book *The Purpose-Driven Life* by Rick Warren. We thought that was worthwhile reading for our senior staff.

Our Christian conviction affects the kind of merchandise we carry and don't carry. For example, you won't find ashtrays at Hobby Lobby, simply because we believe cigarettes are a poor way to take care of the body God created for every human being. You won't find shot glasses; I already spoke in chapter 10 about the dangers of alcohol.

You also won't find off-color, risqué greeting cards—at least you're not supposed to. This is a hard department to control, because the greeting card companies require contracts to replenish the racks directly, and they constantly change their lineups. It works like this: If a customer buys a silver-wedding anniversary card, the card company representative will bring in another silver-wedding anniversary card—but not necessarily the same one that sold. The content is forever changing.

We have made our standards very clear to these suppliers, but sometimes things still slip through the cracks. A customer will buy one of these objectionable cards and send it to me, saying, "Is this what your store really stands for?" I'm ashamed whenever that happens. We go back to the supplier and lodge a complaint, telling them we're going to be watching them more closely in the future.

On another front: We are like many other companies in providing a Christmas bonus to each employee. My son Steve, however, came up with a great idea a while back to include a card with the check. It says:

> Along with this gift of appreciation, it is my hope that you have received the greatest gift ever given, the gift of eternal life. Jesus came to earth to save mankind and offers eternal life to whoever believes in him. If you are unaware of this gift, or want to know more, contact the pastor of a Bible-believing church in your area and ask about the gift of eternal life. This could be the merriest Christmas you've ever had!

This is our way of conveying to our employees what we think is paramount.

We also check ourselves as owners to see if we're honoring the Lord in how we handle assets. Anyone has the right to bring up any issue for examination. One day in the early 1980s, Steve, who had been studying deeply what the Bible says about money and particularly debt, asked us to come to his home for lunch. He said he had some questions to ask.

We had a nice meal together, and then Steve got down to business. "You know, Dad, the book of Proverbs says, 'The borrower is servant to the lender' (22:7). We're up to our eyeballs in debt these days, based on the assumption that if we can borrow money at 7 percent and use it to make profits of 10 percent, or whatever, we'll be ahead of the game. It sounds good—but what if the market doesn't respond the way we think it will?"

I had to admit that Steve had a valid point. Our operating assumption in those days was simply to borrow as much as the bankers would lend us.

What neither he nor I knew was that the crash of 1985 was coming soon. All of a sudden, the market reversed on us, and we were in big trouble. We almost lost everything.

Since then, we have worked to reduce our use of other people's money. As I look back at the history of Hobby Lobby, I really believe if we had not borrowed so much, we would have grown *greater* than we did. That sounds illogical, I know. It's kind of like my other statement that I can be more profitable by closing on Sunday. On the surface, it doesn't make sense—but in fact, history has proved it true. There's a God-factor here that changes normal economics.

I guess a subtle change has occurred over the years in my own attitude. In the early years, I was pretty strongly of the mind-set that said, "If Hobby Lobby is going to be successful, I simply *have to make things happen*!" That meant being aggressive—kicking down doors, so to speak—and insisting on results. I'd tell the real estate department, for example, "We *have* to have such-and-such location. Now make it work!"

I've gone through quite a paradigm change since then. If this is not a "secular" business, I should be able to calm down and lean on the Lord to open doors or close them. I've grown more sensitive to what He might have in mind. I've learned that I don't know the future, and while an opportunity may look good on the front end, the opposite could prove true a year down the road.

I'm not saying I've gone all mellow and placid in managing this organization. I'm still willing to tackle a difficult challenge if necessary. But I am more sensitive to the fact that Someone greater than myself is at work here. I'm not quite the bulldog businessman I used to be.

And the effect on Hobby Lobby as a whole is all for the better, in my view. We are more in sync with the kind of business we are meant to be.

CHAPTER 13

TAKING RISKS

~

Everyone knows the familiar—even trite—slogans about taking risks:

— *Nothing ventured, nothing gained.*

— *He who hesitates is lost.*

— *If the Creator had a purpose in equipping us with a neck, he surely meant for us to stick it out.* (Arthur Koestler)

— *Why not go out on a limb? Isn't that where the fruit is?* (Frank Scully)

Like any entrepreneur, I've taken my share of risks over the years, and I still do. But that doesn't mean I necessarily enjoy it. In fact, I try to minimize the downside possibilities whenever I can. So does any conscientious businessperson.

On the other hand, I know that risk-taking is a necessary component of growing an organization. Let me tell three stories about risk at Hobby Lobby—one from the 1970s, another from the 1980s (that went badly for a while), and a third from just recently.

STARTING FROM SCRATCH

Remember back when five-and-dimes used to have lunch counters? Two of my fellow TG&Y managers and I were sitting at the counter one day having coffee when we got to dreaming about what we might start on our own. I was just twenty-nine years old, and Larry Pico and Jim Stoddard weren't much older.

"Why don't we manufacture clocks?" Larry said. "We could really make a good business out of that."

"Well, if we're going to manufacture something, I have a better idea," I countered. "Small frames—people keep asking for these in our craft department, and I'm having a hard time finding a good supplier."

I wasn't talking about picture frames per se, with glass and matboard and an easel on the back. I was talking about a small frame just three or four inches on a side, with canvas for people who liked to do oil paintings. They would take the canvas out, paint a flower or a windmill or some other object on it, then reassemble the frame and hang it on the wall, often in clusters of five or six.

This was a current surge in arts and crafts in those days. We don't even handle these kinds of frames anymore.

"Hey, that sounds like it could work," one of my friends responded, taking another sip of coffee. "What would we have to buy to get started?"

"Well, the big thing would be a frame chopper, to get the corners right," I said. "Those run several hundred dollars. And then we'd need some wood sticks and canvas."

None of us had any extra money. Barbara and I already had three little kids at home; Mart was nine, Steve was seven, and Darsee was just three. The other managers were in no better shape than I was.

"We'd have to borrow the money," somebody said. "How much would it take?"

"Maybe $600," I estimated. That was about two weeks' pay for guys like us. None of us had that much money lying around, for sure. "We could go to the bank next door here."

At that point, Jim Stoddard began to have cold feet. "I'm not sure about that," he said. "You guys go ahead without me."

In the following days, Larry and I found an equipment supplier in the city named Denton's. There we spotted a Danish-made Morso chopper for $450 that operated by foot power. This was just what we needed to at least make some samples. Add on a selection of molding sticks, glue, clamps, and canvas, and we were indeed looking at about $600 to get started.

At the bank, Larry and I signed a twelve-month loan. They didn't ask us for any collateral; I guess the fact that we both had steady jobs was enough for the bank to take a modest chance on us. Soon we were back at Denton's to buy the machine and the materials. We set them up in Larry's garage, since I had only a carport.

We were too excited to stop and read the instructions. We just started chopping away, which meant we ruined several lengths of molding before we managed to produce anything usable. But soon we had an assortment of attractive miniature frames.

What should we call this bold new enterprise? We couldn't come up with anything more dazzling than a

combination of our two last names: Greco Products (pro-
nounced "*gree*-co")—a name that persists to this day as
one of Hobby Lobby's manufacturing arms.

A salesman from Dallas used to come into my store regularly, selling arts-and-crafts merchandise from various suppliers. The next time he showed up, I said to him, "Hey, let
me show you something my friend and I have started making." I pulled out our samples. "Would you ever be willing
to add these to your lineup and see if you could find some
orders for us as you travel around?"

"Sure, I'll give it a try," he replied. We settled on a commission rate, sent our samples out the door in his case, and
hoped for the best.

Two weeks later, the man returned. "Well, I've got some
business for you!" he announced with a grin. Onto the desk
he laid a total of $3,500 worth of orders from various retail-
ers around Oklahoma and Texas.

This was great! A big smile came across my face. Our
risk was paying off.

But the smile quickly faded as I realized that neither
Larry nor I had any cash with which to buy materials for filling these orders. It was nice to have the business, but if we
couldn't come up with the goods, we were dead.

We didn't know what else to do but take our orders
back to Denton's, lay them out on the table, and plead for
credit. "See, here are the orders we've gotten," we explained
with hopeful faces. "This means we need x feet of molding
from you. Now to get these frames made up, packed and
delivered, and the money collected in order to pay you . . .
it may take longer than thirty days, which we know are
your normal terms. Is there any way you could work with
us on this?"

I can still see Mr. Denton looking at us and then nodding his head. He would be willing to take a chance on these two young fellows. He would give us extended terms. We gleefully went out the door with the supplies we needed.

Soon we were hard at work. We filled the first orders, collected our money, and paid Denton's. Lo and behold, we had $300 left over! Larry Pico wanted to split it between the two of us as profit. But I argued that we needed to reinvest this in more wood to keep the business growing. That's what we did.

We made up a little sales sheet. Barbara did a lot of the frame-making during the day while I was at the TG&Y store in my regular job. We even got our two little sons involved there at the kitchen table; we told them we'd pay them 7 cents for each frame they glued. They jumped at the opportunity to make a little money. Meanwhile, Barbara made almost daily trips to the post office to send out the boxes of frames.

> WE EVEN GOT OUR TWO LITTLE SONS INVOLVED THERE AT THE KITCHEN TABLE; WE TOLD THEM WE'D PAY THEM 7 CENTS FOR EACH FRAME THEY GLUED.

As the months rolled along, volume increased, to the point that she and the boys couldn't keep up with it. Where else could we find workers for an affordable rate? My inventive wife discovered the Cerebral Palsy Center on Portland Avenue near NW Twenty-ninth Street. There she found workers who wanted something to do with their hands. If we'd supply the supervision and training, they would glue frames, insert the canvas, place the product in a plastic bag, and staple our Greco header to the top for 10 cents apiece. It was a win-win for everybody.

Our greater dream was more than this little frame operation, of course. This was just a way to get into retailing for ourselves. If we could accumulate earnings through manufacturing, eventually we could open our own store.

Meanwhile, we kept up with our loan payments to the bank, so that by the end of the year, the $600 was fully returned. This gave us confidence to ask for a second loan. We sat down with the bank representative, described our success so far, and said, "Now we'd like to buy a larger quantity of frame molding, which will give us a better cost of goods. To do that, we need $1,000 this time. Would you be willing to loan us that much?"

To our amazement, they said no! We were too intimidated to argue with them; we instead went slinking out the door and headed down the street to one of their competitors, Union Bank and Trust. There we got a more positive welcome in order to keep growing.

Now I will tell you the name of the first institution. You'll probably recognize it instantly: the infamous Penn Square Bank, which made so many shaky oil-and-gas loans that it collapsed eleven years later (July 1982), endangered bigger partners from Chicago to Seattle, and staggered the whole American banking industry.[1] I subsequently joked to my friends that if Penn Square had only been willing to take a $1,000 risk on us, they would have had at least one good loan to show the auditors!

The business kept growing, and on August 3, 1972, we reached our goal of opening our first retail store. It was tiny, as I said in the first chapter—only 300 square feet. In the back was another 300 square feet that became Greco's manufacturing area.

What would we call this store? Well, again, we didn't have any original ideas. But one of our Greco customers down in Houston had a name with a nice ring to it: "Hobby Lobby." We decided to hang our future on this name, figuring our little operation in Oklahoma City was no threat to them more than 450 miles south. (By the time we expanded into Texas years later, the Houston store was no longer in business.)

Sales for the first month totaled $136.17. That wasn't even enough to pay the monthly rent of $250. Some days there were no customers at all. Darsee, our daughter, remembers sitting on the creaky floor as a kindergartner in those days, playing with beads. She didn't run much risk of getting stepped on.

But we hung in there, saw the volume begin to build, and then the Christmas season came along. We ended the year with $3,200 in gross sales. A couple of months later we moved to a larger house and kept expanding.

The year 1973 picked up strongly for us. By September Larry and I realized we weren't quite on the same wavelength, and perhaps it would be better for us to split up. Sitting in a McDonald's one morning, I bought him out for $5,000, and since then Greco has been in one set of hands.

By the end of 1974, our second full year of business, we found we had grossed $150,000 and cleared a $36,000 profit. We had found a bright young partner named John Seward, a talented artist who ran our store in the beginning and gave creative direction to our arts and crafts, while Barbara kept boxing shipments of frames in the back. We couldn't pay John what he was worth, so we gave him part ownership of the business instead—an arrangement that persisted until 1994.

Meanwhile, I was thinking even more seriously about leaving my position at TG&Y and taking the big leap for myself. Yes, it was a scary thought. It would mean giving up a guaranteed $26,000-a-year salary in a $2 billion company. I could see that our new little operation could pay me only half that much: $13,000 a year.

But one of my supervisors had said to me once, "David, do you know what's different about you compared to all the other managers?"

"No, what?"

"Confidence," he replied.

Barbara and I prayed about this bold step and decided to go for it. It was not so much a matter of expecting to become prosperous as it was a sense of providence: This was what God meant for us to do. I know that probably sounds strange to a lot of people, but down inside, we felt sure about this move.

> I WAS OWNER, BOOKKEEPER, JANITOR, THE GUY WHO BUILT THE HOMEMADE COUNTERS OUT OF TWO-BY-FOURS AND ONE-BY-TWELVES—YOU NAME IT.

In March 1975, I turned in my resignation, and we opened our second store. I plunged full-force into Greco and Hobby Lobby. I was owner, bookkeeper, janitor, the guy who built the homemade counters out of two-by-fours and one-by-twelves—you name it. Barbara gave as much time as she could while still being a faithful mom. Viola Howell was our first full-time salesclerk.

Total sales at the end of that year were $742,261. We were on our way. Our risk had paid off.

Risking is different from gambling, although people often confuse the two terms. When you gamble, you have no influence over the outcome. Somebody just buys a lottery ticket and hopes for good luck. The buyer can do nothing to affect the result.

When you risk, you can control at least *some* factors. You have a hand in your destiny. People come to me wanting to enter the retail world and ask my advice. I say, "Okay, write down all the 'knowns.' How much rent will you have to pay for a store? How much for utilities? How much for wages? What are your margins?" They start putting these numbers together.

The unknown, of course, is how many sales they will actually get. They can give an educated guess, but they won't know for sure until they open the doors for business. So that's the risk factor. But having gone through the exercise of declaring the known expenses, they're in better shape to understand the business and whether it might succeed.

OUT OF OUR LEAGUE

My next story of risk is not nearly so pleasant. That's because I stuck my neck out unconsciously, without studying the situation in advance and making a careful assessment. Before I knew it, I was in deep trouble.

As I mentioned in chapter 2, our regional economy was fairly cooking in the early 1980s. The oil business was booming, and money was flowing freely. Mercedes-Benz and

Rolls-Royce dealers were selling every car they could get their hands on. Rolex watches were flying out the doors of the jewelry stores. You'd hear stories about people giving $100 tips to restaurant waiters, golf caddies, or bell captains at hotels.

At Hobby Lobby, we got swept up in the excitement, I'm afraid. We had been born as an arts-and-crafts store, but now we were loading up on expensive cookware, gourmet foods such as bird's nest soup, signed and numbered artwork that sold for thousands, collector dolls—all kinds of upscale merchandise. We were coasting high on a false sense of security. We were playing in a bigger league than we realized.

Then suddenly—oil prices began to drop. Energy companies began laying people off. Penn Square Bank fell with a loud thud. At the same time, the price of beef began slipping, which hurt cattle ranchers. All this meant that tax revenues skidded, and state government had to tighten its belt. The Oklahoma legislature passed the largest tax increase in its history.

And, of course, customers realized that the fancy ceiling fan at Hobby Lobby wasn't nearly as essential as it had seemed a few months before. Our high-ticket merchandise was just sitting there going nowhere. Sales revenues plummeted. It almost seemed as if I woke up one morning, and the party was over.

We were stuck with more than $100,000 worth of twist beads alone. I couldn't pay vendors. We began slashing prices right and left just to move product and garner a little cash. The margins were pitiful. I found myself spending more and more time with bankers pleading for loans. One, sensing my desperation, was willing to loan me $200,000— but diverted $40,000 of that into a non-interest-bearing CD right off the top. So I got only $160,000 to use, while paying interest on the whole amount.

> ## WE WERE STUCK WITH MORE THAN $100,000 WORTH OF TWIST BEADS ALONE. I COULDN'T PAY VENDORS.

By then we had twelve Hobby Lobby stores plus other affiliate corporations such as Greco, and I had always assumed that this diversity would be our salvation. If one company lost money, the others would pick up the slack. But it seemed all the companies were bleeding cash at once.

I didn't know how bad it was until, in early 1986, we completed inventory for the previous calendar year. Suddenly, there were the ugly facts right in front of me: $25 million in sales for the year, and a bottom-line loss of almost $1 million. We had *never* lost money any previous year. I knew I was in major trouble.

Mike Henry, assistant manager of our Tenth Street store, remembers the morning he saw all his cashiers huddled at the front of the store.

"What's up?" he asked as he approached them. "What's going on?"

"OG&E [Oklahoma Gas and Electric] is here to cut off the electricity," the head cashier answered with downcast eyes.

Mike gasped and turned to the utility workers, ushering them off to the side so customers wouldn't hear the conversation. They told him he'd have to come up with $3,600 immediately, or else the power was going off.

Mike scrambled for a solution. He knew he didn't have that much cash in the store. "Can you give me until tomorrow?" he begged. "I expect a good day in sales today, and we'll pay you cash in the morning."

"No, I'm sorry, but we can't do that."

"Look," Mike persisted, "I'm a neighbor of yours. You know I'm not going anywhere. You know Hobby Lobby. I'll be right here with the money, I promise."

With that, the OG&E man relented. And the next day, Mike was able to produce the $3,600.

He felt too awkward to tell me the story directly. But the company comptroller found out and was not a happy man. He had planned to use that day's receipts to pay other creditors.

On another afternoon, the city water department did actually cut off the Tenth Street store's water. Mike quickly ran over to the city office and paid the bill temporarily out of his own pocket to get service restored.

At the home office, things were just as tense. We cut workers' hours wherever we could. All raises were put on hold. We decided we would save fuel by sending trucks out to the stores with new merchandise only half as often, every two weeks instead of weekly as we had always done (and still do today). But this, of course, meant more empty shelves, which hurt sales even further. It was a chicken-and-egg dilemma: We needed more sales, but that meant bringing in more goods, and the vendors were not going to ship us any more until we paid for the previous batch.

It seemed like nothing I tried would work. My nerves were shot. Every time the phone rang, I knew it would be another creditor wanting payment. I was toast. Some nights I doubt if I slept a total of one hour.

The only thing I knew to do was pray, "God, what do you want me to learn from this?" I would leave the office sometimes and walk alone in Eldon Lyons Park, crying out for help and guidance. Other times, I would literally crawl down under my desk to plead with God. It was a way of getting alone for prayer without people watching me.

Barbara tried to comfort me those days by saying, "David, it's God's business. If he takes it away, we'll do something else." That was true; I knew I could get another job someplace in retail and put food on the table. But what about my kids, all three of whom were employed in the company? What about my two nephews, Jeff and Randy, whom we had helped to raise and now employed as well? What about all the other faithful workers? It was awful.

Then came the dramatic family meeting in April 1986 that I described in chapter 2. I laid out the ugly facts. I said I thought we could still turn this around by getting back to our core business, but maybe not in time. That was when Mart, our oldest son, made his epic statement about "our faith is not in you, Dad; it's in God."

Steve, our other son, added, "Whatever happens, Dad, we love you."

Stan Lett, Darsee's fiancé who had worked for us since high school, added, "You're not responsible for our future. We'll make it somehow."

In time, our downsizing and cost-cutting began to show results, and the monthly profit returned. We started coming out of the dark tunnel. I could tell we were stabilizing. Through it all, I had learned that I had to become small so God could be big. He was preparing me for the rest of my life.

Up until this time, I had always given God credit for our

success, but I'm afraid it was mostly lip service. Now I saw where I could truly wind up without God's help.

> UP UNTIL THIS TIME, I HAD ALWAYS GIVEN GOD CREDIT FOR OUR SUCCESS, BUT I'M AFRAID IT WAS MOSTLY LIP SERVICE. NOW I SAW WHERE I COULD TRULY WIND UP WITHOUT GOD'S HELP.

I would like to be able to say that I was a strong leader at the helm of the ship through this storm. But that wouldn't be true. Barbara, in fact, was stronger than I was. We both just did what we knew to do and prayed like crazy.

I could tell we were doing better financially on a day-to-day basis. But we were still seriously behind on our loans. The day came in November 1986 when a letter was delivered by hand from the president of our bank. We owed them about $1.3 million. The wording was definitely stiff:

Reference is made to that certain promissory note number 64477 dated June 1, 1986 . . .

As you know, you have failed to comply with the terms of the note, and the same is in default. Demand is made for immediate and full payment on the indebtedness.

This Bank will exercise all of its legal rights if payment is not made at this time.

I shuddered when I read that last paragraph. They were threatening to foreclose on everything we owned.

I immediately began looking for a different bank.

Fortunately, Bank of Oklahoma was willing to look at us. We moved our accounts there, borrowed enough to pay off the other bank, and when the books were closed for 1986, we had *made* $1.2 million in contrast to the loss of the year before. We were back on our feet. We've stayed in the black every year since then.

I don't know if the bank truly intended to lock us up or not. Maybe that was just its way of letting us know it would prefer to not have us as a customer. Anyway, after we recovered, I took that letter, framed it, and hung it in the entryway of our home office as a reminder of what we had survived. It stayed there for many years.

But then one night, I felt a twinge of unease about that. It was as if God was saying to me, *Why are you displaying that letter? What's your motive? Is it to show off a little now that you're successful and stable? It's kind of a na-na-n'-nana, isn't it?*

You need to take that down from the wall.

I did exactly that the very next morning when I went into the office.

And would you believe, *the following week*, that bank president's wife was killed in a car accident! I was shocked at the tragedy, and even more so at the timing of God's nudge to me. The lesson I gathered was that I should not have been taunting that man in any way, however subtle. It wasn't respectful.

God cares far more about our hearts than he does our profits. We are dependent on him for the next breath we take. I believe that whenever I consider taking a risk in business, I dare not leave him out of the equation. What he thinks is what I desperately need to know. Otherwise, I can get in huge trouble.

TODAY'S CHALLENGE

Various other stretches have come our way in the intervening years. That's just the nature of business. I tend to get a little wide-eyed every time we commit to building an additional warehouse. The first one was just 87,000 square feet, and I said to myself, "Well, that's a lot of space; we'll need to sublet half of it." But before long we needed the whole thing.

Ever since, it seems we're always behind in providing warehouse space. Another half-million square feet always seem to be on the drawing board. At the time of this writing, we're up to three million square feet—and we're still renting another 100,000 in another building.

Some of the warehouse need has been driven by a new venture we launched in the fall of 2001, an upscale furnishings store called Hemispheres. In traveling overseas, we kept seeing really nice merchandise that we knew a certain level of customer would like. Yes, it was expensive. But it was also attractive.

And we'd say to one another, "Okay, but this is definitely not Hobby Lobby." We certainly didn't want to repeat our mistakes from the early 1980s.

So after considerable study and prayer, we took on a whole different model: a home *furnishings* store. That's not the same as a furniture store. Whereas a standard furniture store would have a few mirrors displayed in its various vignettes, we have row upon row of nice mirrors, lamps, exquisite beds and bedcoverings, lavish garden fountains, lawn furniture, containers for outdoor plants, hand-knotted rugs, and so on. As one of our managers told a reporter, "When you start shopping here, you'll travel through more than thirty countries." If you're moving into a new home, you can come to Hemispheres and pretty much take care of all the furnishings you want.

We felt that as Hobby Lobby filled its niche in all the feasible cities we wanted to enter, we needed another, different vehicle for growth. But we didn't want to overreach and take on too much risk all at once. So we opened five stores for starters: one in Oklahoma City, three in the Dallas area, and one in St. Louis. We needed the volume of five to get the efficiency of importing full containerloads from Asia and elsewhere.

Are we profitable yet? No. But we're getting better at what we do. We're learning what works and what doesn't. Each store's volume is increasing year after year, sometimes as high as 32 percent. I foresee us breaking into the black in another couple of years.

Granted, this kind of operation is more vulnerable to the national economy than is Hobby Lobby. These customers are more likely to be active in the stock market, for example. If their investments start losing, they'll pull back from buying nice furnishings. Hobby Lobby, on the other hand, seems pretty much recession-proof. In fact, when economic times are bad, people tend to start making and crafting even more of their gifts instead of buying them ready-made. They do more "nesting," it seems, which is good for us.

So Hemispheres is a different kind of risk. I can't guarantee that it's going to be a roaring success. But I'm not intimidated by that. If it goes well and grows—as I think it will—I'll be pleased and will try to be a good steward of its potential.

Risk is part of life. And I believe that if my life is entrusted to God's care and guidance, he will help me handle the risk that goes with it.

CHAPTER 14

So What?

~ ∽ ~

By now I hope you've caught the idea that I don't view the retailing of flowers and frames and flannel as the most important thing in the world. It is a decent and honorable way to make a living—and to provide employees with a way to make a living. It provides attractive and useful products to the buying public. I'm glad to be doing it. But it's not going to win the Nobel Peace Prize, or find a cure for cancer, or earn a gold mansion in heaven.

On the other hand, I've given a fair amount of thought during the years to the deeper questions of purpose. What's my real reason for doing what I do? What gets me up in the morning to face another day?

In the beginning, my goals weren't very profound. Shortly before my wedding (at the tender age of nineteen), I outlined three simple ambitions for my future:

1. To build a happy marriage
2. To raise healthy, well-balanced children who would serve God
3. To succeed in business

That's all. With those goals in mind, I moved forward with Barbara at my side.

When I was promoted to store manager at the age of twenty-one, making $100 a week, I was excited. We were on our way to utopia! I remember coming home and telling my mother, "Hey, Mom, guess what—I just made store manager. I'm one of the youngest guys they've ever put in this position."

She smiled and then said quietly, "That's nice, Dave. But what are you doing for the Lord?"

That was a touchy question for me, given the fact that I was the only one of the six Green children who was *not* going into the ordained ministry. My father, as I have mentioned, was a pastor, and my two brothers were following in his footsteps. Two sisters had married pastors, and the third became an evangelist. I felt like the black sheep of the family.

Nobody said anything directly to me about this, but I got the message anyway: I was chasing the almighty dollar, trying to be a capitalist, messing around without true purpose in my life. A well-known devotional poem in our house had always been this:

Only one life; 'twill soon be past.
Only what's done for Christ will last.

The trouble was, God had not gifted me to be a minister. I wasn't a good speaker or singer. I was uneasy with crowds, in fact. I had only one talent, it seemed: making a retail store work properly.

So that's what I kept doing. Barbara and I went to church regularly, and we honored the Lord in the way we lived. When our children came along, we taught them to love God too. But we didn't see any way to go beyond that.

A few years later, I was able to say once again, "Hey, Mom—I just got another promotion. I'm district manager now over twenty stores!"

And again she smiled and replied, "That's very good, Dave. But what are you doing for the Lord?"

I didn't resent her for this. I wanted to please God the way she had taught me from childhood on up. I just didn't know what shape that might take.

My mother passed away in 1975, just as I was leaving TG&Y to give full attention to this new business. She never saw what Hobby Lobby would become.

STEPPING OUT TO GIVE

Three or four years after her death, I was attending a large convention of our church in Tennessee. Missionaries from all over the world gave presentations on their work. I paid close attention, remembering how my mother had always given special care and effort to mission funding.

Flying home after the meetings ended, I was looking out the airplane window when something unusual happened. It seemed that a quiet voice inside my spirit said, *You need to give $30,000 for literature.* One of the speakers had talked about the need for more printed material in his particular field.

My first reaction on the plane was that this was far too much money to consider. The company wasn't nearly big enough to afford this. Where had that number even come from, anyway? Impossible . . .

But the impression wouldn't go away.

God, I don't have $30,000, I silently prayed. *But . . . you're serious about this, aren't you? Well—I suppose I could write four checks for $7,500 each, and postdate them a month apart for the next four months.*

I sat there pondering this option. I did some calculating in my head. Maybe this would work after all.

When I reached home, that is what I did. I put the four checks in an envelope, took a deep breath, prayed that I could make good on them, and mailed them back to Tennessee.

When the church official on the other end called to acknowledge my gift, he made an intriguing comment. "The very day your letter was postmarked," he said, "was the same day that four African missionaries had a special prayer meeting for literature funds. Looks like God answered their prayer!"

Something clicked inside me at that moment. *Maybe God has a purpose for a merchant after all. Maybe he has a place for me.*

SOMETHING CLICKED INSIDE ME AT THAT MOMENT. MAYBE GOD HAS A PURPOSE FOR A MERCHANT AFTER ALL. MAYBE HE HAS A PLACE FOR ME.

I am happy to be able to report that we made good on all four of those checks. It wasn't easy. But the dollars worked out in the end. And I had been stretched in a good direction.

A few years later, a different kind of avenue opened for

making a difference in people's lives. We began Mardel Christian & Educational Supply. This became my oldest son's project (the name comes from "Mart DeLyn," his first and middle names). He had already worked for Hobby Lobby during high school and had shown his aptitude for math.

I was glad to support him in an enterprise of his own. In 1981 we found a 7,000-square-foot space in the Springdale Shopping Center in northwest Oklahoma City that would be ideal—except that it was too big. So I suggested he add office supplies to his business, making a combination store. In those days, Office Depot and Staples hadn't yet arrived on the scene, and most businesses had to order their supplies through salespeople who came around. We thought office people might like to run down to a retail store for their padded envelopes and file folders instead.

There were other Christian bookstores in our city, but none carried the breadth of product that Mardel would provide. Just as Hobby Lobby was known for its amazing selection, Mardel would offer an impressive array of Christian books, music, and gifts. In another section would be the office supplies, and a third section would offer educational materials. Thus the customer had three reasons to stop at our store.

Mart grossed $18,000 in the first month of operation. The second month brought in $34,000, and by December, sales hit $91,000.

We saw the potential right away. This growth curve was even steeper than the early days of Hobby Lobby. "Let's get busy and open a second store," we said to each other.

Today the chain consists of nineteen stores in six states averaging $3.5 million a year each. They have become a major contributor to our family of companies. Throughout the Christian products industry, Mardel is hailed for its pacesetting performance.

Another venture, a more recent one, is a movie company, Every Tribe Entertainment, whose first feature-length film was *End of the Spear*. It's the dramatic documentary of the Waodani tribe (formerly called Aucas) in the remote jungles of Ecuador that slaughtered five missionaries back in 1956, but have since come to accept the Christian message. As a result, they no longer hack and stab one another to death as in the past. A whole culture has been brought to peace and health.

The second film will be a thriller based in China, featuring an eight-year-old boy whose father has been arrested for his work as a pastor. The theme will be resilience in the face of pressure.

We have high hopes for what this company will accomplish.

GOALS THAT MATTER

As the organization kept growing throughout the 1980s, I would periodically update my goals, adding more specifics. For example, when we had four or five Hobby Lobby stores up and running, I said, "I want to get to thirty stores, each of them doing $2.5 million a year in sales volume. Wouldn't that be great?"

Well, that day came in 1991. But well before that, I had changed the marker to a new and bigger figure. I never wanted to arrive at a goal and then look around, saying, "Now what?" I intended to always be stretching toward something greater.

But as the years went by, I found that the question of "Now what?" began to shift toward a different question: "So what?" The process was getting repetitive. Would I spend my entire life just reaching toward bigger numbers with more zeros at the end?

In a sense, I had reached my initial trio of goals. My marriage to Barbara was great, the three kids were doing very well, and the business was healthy. So what? I was facing the need for a transition from *success* to *significance*.

In the last ten years or so, two new goals have come into focus in my life.

One is to do everything I can to see that my *grand*children grow up to love and serve God. We have sixteen altogether (actually, that includes seven grandnieces and grandnephews, the children of our two nephews, Jeff and Randy). I can't control this younger generation's life choices any more than I could engineer our own children's choices. But I can show them the example of what it means to live for Christ, and I can pray for them unceasingly.

I can also, by the way, keep them levelheaded in the midst of Hobby Lobby's success. God didn't put any of us here, I tell them, to sit on a yacht. They are welcome to be involved in the company just as their parents are, but they will get only what they earn. We're determined to be careful stewards of this third generation and not let our successes warp their view of the hard work that life requires.

The second goal of my life that has become central is to use my resources to present Christ to as many people as I can. Actually, I shouldn't say "my"—I should say "our"—because this is the passion of Barbara and our children and our nephews as well; together, we make up the board of directors. Once a month we gather to look at our earnings and decide as a group how much to give to various projects. It's one of the truly rewarding things we get to do.

In order to keep giving, we need to keep growing Hobby Lobby and its affiliate companies. This is what energizes my day-to-day work in retailing now—the knowledge that if we can add stores and thereby boost profits, we can give away that much more to make a difference eternally. I'll *definitely* get out of bed in the morning to see that happen!

We don't make a lot of noise about the specific programs to which we give, for obvious reasons. Some of them are local here in Oklahoma City. Others are far away on other continents. We watch carefully to make sure they handle the funds responsibly and touch people's lives in the way they said they would. And we celebrate the results together.

Inside the company, we do share some of the details with our various managers. In fact, we sometimes hear from them, "You guys ought to tell us more about what you're giving. We're a part of this too." So we've put up a few charts and photos. But we remain pretty careful about this. Jesus once said it's better when the left hand doesn't even know what the right hand is giving (Matthew 6:3), and we try to stick close to that principle.

Businesspeople have said to me, "When are you going to take Hobby Lobby public? You could float quite a stock offering, you know." Yes, I suppose so. But I'm not interested. For one thing, we don't need the additional cash these days; we're able to grow as fast as we want. And second, I don't want to have to debate with stockholders about what we do with the profits. The family and I want to stay free to run the holiday message ads, to pay for a hospital in Haiti, to support our local City Rescue Mission that serves the homeless downtown, to print the sixty-four-page *Book of Hope* (a biography of Jesus condensed from the four Gospels) for people in faraway places who are curious about him.

This is what gives us joy.

THE WEAK, THE STRONG

I realize a lot of business leaders may disagree with me, but I truly believe that God belongs in what my company does. By putting him first in my operation, he can bless what I attempt. He doesn't want me to think I'm so intelligent that I can run this place without him. When I admit my weakness, he seizes the opportunity to be strong.

More than once I've gone home at night with two or three problems weighing on my mind. I haven't known what to do about them. Usually, I'm a pretty decisive guy; I call the shot (even if it's wrong!), and we move forward. But sometimes, I can see a lot of complications, and I know not to get in too big a hurry in those cases.

That's when I'll take some evening time to pray about it. Sometimes I'll ask Barbara to join me, and we'll pray together for wisdom. By the next morning, I'll have a sense in my mind of what to do. I'll drive to the office with confidence.

The prophet Isaiah said, "As the heavens are higher than the earth, so are [God's] ways higher than your ways and [God's] thoughts than your thoughts."[1] He has answers I would never come up with on my own. He sees issues and factors that escape me entirely.

I've found over the years that I need to consult with him constantly—not just when things are falling apart. Crisis prayer is okay, but daily prayer is even better. It's kind of sad when people say, "The situation was so bad the only thing we could do was pray." Why not pray before it gets that bad?

There is a God, and he's not averse to business. He's not just a "Sunday deity." He understands margins and spreadsheets, competition and profits. I appreciate the open door to discuss all those things with him, and to see what he can accomplish through ordinary retailing.

> **THERE IS A GOD, AND HE'S NOT AVERSE TO BUSINESS. HE'S NOT JUST A "SUNDAY DEITY." HE UNDERSTANDS MARGINS AND SPREADSHEETS, COMPETITION AND PROFITS.**

Pleasing customers is important, but pleasing God through the way I run the business is even more important.

BACK TO ALTUS

I got a chance to talk about this not long ago, when my hometown school superintendent asked me to come back to my roots and address his staff during a kickoff orientation day before classes resumed in the fall. I don't accept most speaking invitations, because it's not my talent. But for this, I said yes.

Barbara and I had not been back to this county-seat town in the southwest corner of the state for a long time. We drove the 150 miles the afternoon before, so we'd have time just to look around, remembering how and where we met. We drove by her old home as well as the tiny church my dad had pastored.

The next morning, in the auditorium of the high school from which I had barely graduated, I stood up to face 350 teachers plus another 150 support staff. A few of my teachers were still present, now nearing retirement. I started off by thanking them for what their profession had invested in the life of a shy kid from the other side of the tracks. One teacher, I recalled, had given me a pair of shoes. I told about the woman who coaxed her electrician husband into giving me an after-school job as his gofer. An English teacher, realizing I was far behind, had taken me across the hall to an empty room and matched me with the sharpest student she had, who tutored me so I could catch up.

I recounted a very kind junior high teacher of Oklahoma history who used to help us during quizzes with little hints. The question that day was: "When the early cattlemen drove their herds up the western branch of the Chisholm Trail, they eventually arrived in what Kansas 'city'?" She emphasized the last word in such a way that we all knew the answer included that word. And with her body, she began pantomiming the other word by crouching down and feinting back and forth with her head and arms, almost like a charade.

Kids quickly got the idea and wrote down their answers. I wasn't quite sure, but I took a guess. The next day, she gave the results. "On question seven, everybody in the class got it right except one," she said. "Dodge City, of course, was the end of the western branch of the Chisholm Trail. But we did have one person who wrote, 'Duck City.'"

When my audience finally stopped laughing, I dropped my voice and continued, "That person is your speaker today. Now you know why the emcee told you I was accepting no honorarium for this speech. I wanted you to get your money's worth."

Eventually, I moved along to my main theme: Life is like a vapor; it passes away all too quickly. Temporal things don't last. Only the eternal things endure.

"Last evening Barbara and I went down to the square and walked around once more," I told them. "McClellan's five-and-dime, where we got our start in retail, isn't there anymore. That building is now a law office. Woolworth's, our main competitor back then, is gone as well. Both of the drugstores from my growing-up years are out of business now. The Sagamore Hotel, where my sisters worked in the number one restaurant in town, isn't there either."

The crowd buzzed with people remembering those landmarks from the past.

"But that's the way our temporal life is. Someday, Hobby Lobby will be gone as well. It, too, is just a vapor. Institutions rise and fall. What counts for eternity, on the other hand, is a whole different matter.

> **INSTITUTIONS RISE AND FALL. WHAT COUNTS FOR ETERNITY, ON THE OTHER HAND, IS A WHOLE DIFFERENT MATTER.**

"As you go into this school year, think about how you can affect your students in an eternal sense, not just a temporal one. Yes, there are limitations on what can be said in a public school. But why not focus on what *can* be done rather than what can't? You and I have the opportunity every day to shape the future for a long, long time."

More than one person came up to thank me afterward.

"What you said is going to make a difference in how I teach this year," said one man.

The truth is, whether you and I are in education or retailing, in government or private industry, a public figure or a full-time homemaker, the "So what?" question of life is vitally important. Some things will matter forever, while others will fade in less than a week. Figuring out which is which—and then doing something about it—is a task not to be overlooked.

The measure of my life, and yours, is not how much money we accumulate or how many trophies we collect. It is rather the way in which we align ourselves with God's purposes, and thereby impact eternity. In other words, all this daily activity that so consumes us—it's meant to be more than a hobby, or even a career. We are here on this planet for a serious reason. Whatever time is left, I intend to make the most of it.

A FAMILY OF COMPANIES

Hobby Lobby is the largest privately owned arts-and-crafts retailer in the world. It operates more than 300 stores in 27 American states: Alabama, Arkansas, Colorado, Florida, Georgia, Illinois, Indiana, Iowa, Kansas, Kentucky, Louisiana, Michigan, Minnesota, Mississippi, Missouri, Nebraska, New Mexico, North Carolina, North Dakota, Ohio, Oklahoma, South Carolina, South Dakota, Tennessee, Texas, Wisconsin, and Wyoming. It opens a new store about every two weeks. See www.hobbylobby.com.

In addition:

Mardel Christian & Educational Supply is a nineteen-store chain that retails Christian materials, office supplies, and educational materials. Its stores are in Arkansas, Colorado, Kansas, Missouri, Oklahoma, and Texas. See www.mardel.com.

Hemispheres opened its doors in September 2001 and currently has five showrooms in Missouri, Oklahoma, and Texas. It specializes in the unique and luxurious comforts of home from around the world.

See www.hemispheres-us.com.

Crafts, Etc.! is a packager and distributor of domestic and imported arts, crafts, jewelry-making and hobby merchandise, not only to Hobby Lobby but also to other retail customers. It also sells more than 20,000 items directly to customers through the Internet. See www.craftsetc.com.

Worldwood was established in 1988 to manufacture our store fixtures. It has since added a line of unfinished wood décor items as well as throw pillows and stretched canvas frames. The most recent division, Endless Possibilities, manufactures potpourri, candles, and scents.

See www.world-wood.com.

Basket Market is a bulk-sales store that serves Oklahoma City floral shops.

Greco Frame & Supply manufactures custom and ready-made frames and mats.

H. L. Realty is responsible for property management throughout the companies.

Bearing Fruit Entertainment is a nonprofit communications company that promotes the relevance of God's Word through advertising and filmmaking.

See www.bearingfruit.org.

Every Tribe Entertainment is a for-profit film company that specializes in dramatic stories from cultures around the world.

Isle Connection is a sourcing and buying office in the Philippines.

Hong Kong Connection is a sourcing and buying office in China.

NOTES

CHAPTER 4

1. Linda Babcock and Sara Laschever, *Women Don't Ask: Negotiation and the Gender Divide* (Princeton, N.J.: Princeton University Press, 2003).

CHAPTER 6

1. Al Ries and Jack Trout, *The 22 Immutable Laws of Marketing* (New York: Harper Business, 1993), 96–97.

CHAPTER 9

1. "Do not have two differing weights in your bag—one heavy, one light. Do not have two differing measures in your house—one large, one small. You must have accurate and honest weights and measures, so that you may live long in the land the LORD your God is giving you. For the LORD your God detests anyone who does these things, anyone who deals dishonestly" (Deuteronomy 25:13–16).

2. "Do not withhold good from those who deserve it, when it is in your power to act. Do not say to your neighbor, 'Come back later; I'll give it tomorrow'—when you now have it with you" (Proverbs 3:27–28); "Let no debt remain outstanding, except the continuing debt to love one another, for he who loves his fellowman has fulfilled the law" (Romans 13:8).

3. Roy P. Basler, ed., "Notes for a Law Lecture," *The Collected Works of Abraham Lincoln* (New Brunswick, N.J.: Rutgers University Press, 1953), vol. II, 81.

CHAPTER 10

1. "The Power of Seven," *Economist*, 20 December 2001.

2. Nan Chase, "Ancient Wisdom," *Hemispheres*, July 1997, 118–19.

3. Susan Brink, "The Price of Booze," *U.S. News & World Report*, 2 February 2004, 48–50.

CHAPTER 11

1. Dorothy Sayers, "Why Work?" Letters to a Diminished Church (Nashville: W Publishing, 2004), 139.

2. John W. Gardner, *Excellence: Can We Be Equal and Excellent Too?* (New York: HarperCollins, 1961).

CHAPTER 13

1. For the full story, see *Wall Street Journal* reporter Phillip L. Zweig's *Belly Up: The Collapse of the Penn Square Bank* (New York: Crown, 1985), or Mark Singer's *Funny Money* (New York: Knopf, 1985).

CHAPTER 14

1. Isaiah 55:9.

About the Authors

—— ∽ ——

David Green is founder of Hobby Lobby. Born into a pastor's home, he began working at a local five-and-dime as a teen. After he married his high school sweetheart, the young couple began a small picture-frame shop. In 1972 they opened their first retail store. Today Hobby Lobby has more than 300 stores in 27 states. David and his wife, Barbara, have three grown children.

Dean Merrill is best known in recent years for his collaborations with Jim Cymbala (*Fresh Wind, Fresh Fire* and its two sequels) and Philippine missionary survivor Gracia Burnham (*In the Presence of My Enemies*). He is a former president of the Evangelical Press Association and a recognized editorial mentor from his years at *Campus Life* magazine, *Leadership Journal* (CTI), *Christian Herald,* and Focus on the Family. Merrill is married and the father of three.

If you enjoyed *More Than a Hobby,* by David Green, consider these other quality business titles from Nelson Business:

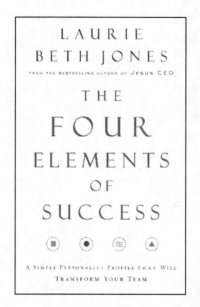

THE FOUR ELEMENTS OF SUCCESS

Small businesses, large corporations, churches, and organizations of all sizes need to have an easily understood method for hiring, placement, team building, and personnel integration so that all members in the organizational ladder can be at their effective best. *New York Times* best-selling author Laurie Beth Jones developed the Path Elements Profile (PEP), which can be used in recruitment, placement, retention, team building, and customer relations. Based upon the elements of Earth, Water, Wind, and Fire, *The Four Elements of Success* will help leaders determine both individual and team behavioral tendencies that affect everything. INCLUDES an assessment test for your team's elemental strengths and weaknesses.

ISBN: 0-7852-0888-7

THOMAS NELSON
Since 1798

thomasnelson.com

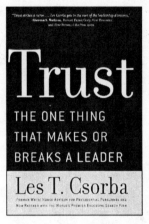

TRUST

From the perspective of someone who served a U.S. president, a U.S. senator, and a governor, author Les T. Csorba sees trust as the most indispensable force between leaders and followers. In *Trust* he offers observations gleaned from two decades of experience in government, business, church, and family. The book features interactive elements such as a guide to evaluating whether you are developing the trust necessary to motivate and richly lead followers.

ISBN 0-7852-6154-0

AESOP & THE CEO

David Noonan, in a clever melding of modern business sense and ancient wisdom, uses the ancient fables of Aesop as a backdrop for 50 significant lessons from the greatest business leaders of our day. Both entertaining and informative, *Aesop & the CEO* is comprised of short, easy-to-read vignettes that cover every aspect of corporate life: negotiations, hiring and firing, mergers and acquisitions, marketing and sales, and day-to-day management.

ISBN 0-7852-6010-2

THOMAS NELSON
Since 1798

thomasnelson.com

Sales quotas, stress-filled days, and long working hours fill the schedules of salespeople everywhere. But that formula is all wrong, says Todd Duncan. Instead he tells us how we can have more sales with less stress, more family time with less frustration, and more money with less work time.

Productivity. It has been a buzz word in the business world for years. But despite our best attempts and countless self-help books, we still fall behind, work late, juggle our schedules, and become swamped. *Time Traps* addresses the most common misconceptions we have about time and our use of that time in the marketplace. Duncan has proven remedies for universal time troubles, and he shows readers how to set a schedule that works not just some days but every day. With the principles in *Time Traps*, salespeople will see a rise in their sales as they experience a drop in their working hours.

ISBN: 0-7852-6323-3

THOMAS NELSON
Since 1798

thomasnelson.com

LaVergne, TN USA
25 March 2011
221628LV00001B/1/P